MW00617148

Growing to Love God's Word

An In-Depth Study of Psalm 119

Joseph Davis

Sermon to Book

Growing to Love God's Word / Joseph Davis
ISBN-13: 978-1-945793-96-7

I first want to thank my beloved high school English teacher, Marlene Larson, now with her Savior in Heaven. The lessons you taught me about writing—and following Jesus—echo loudly in my heart and mind to this day. To Marlene's husband Eric—my high school principal—words cannot express the level of affection I have for you, my dear brother. This book is written in honor of you both.

I also want to dedicate this book to all the young people who were part of my first full-time youth pastor position at Three Rivers Baptist Church in Irmo, South Carolina in the mid-1990s. We went through Psalm 119 together as I taught you what I was learning each week. To this day many of you express how those times together shaped your lifetime relationship with God's Word.

I also would like to thank Tom Fillinger, founder of IgniteUS, who was the executive pastor at Three Rivers Baptist when I was there. Your daily affirmation and encouragement to continue to pursue my study of Psalm 119 meant more to me as a young pastor than you will ever know.

Next is my dear friend and mentor David Barker, who first introduced me to Psalm 119 nearly thirty years ago and convinced me that it could change my life. Dave, you were so right! I have never been the same since!

Next, I want to tell my congregation at GraceLife Sarasota how much I love you all. Your support has been crucial to this project. I don't know where our family would be without you all. We love you so much.

Lastly, I want to thank my family for carrying the burden of being a pastor's family.

CONTENTS

Foreword by Dr. Samkon Gado

I had the amazing privilege of growing up in a God-fearing home with two parents who loved the Lord and each other. It was common for us to come together as a family for evening devotions. However, during the elementary years of my youth, I never saw the value of reading God's Word, but instead saw it as something I was supposed to do. I can't ever remember reading God's Word on my own initiative. In addition, the times I participated corporately, it didn't feel like a life-giving exercise. This continued until middle school, when I became part of the youth group at our church and met Pastor Joe.

Joe was the new youth pastor from Florida who had a pretty decent basketball shot and moved surprisingly well for a man his size. He was much heavier back then. However, his deceptive athleticism excluded the most defining mark of Pastor Joe—his genuine desire for the Lord and His Word. He had a sincere yearning for his youth group to see the beauty of the Lord through a diligent relationship with His Word. I distinctly remember our weekly gatherings were consistently marked by an in depth look at Christ through the Word. To this day, I remember Joe pleading with us from his black music stand in a double-wide trailer as he poured over the Scriptures. It was clear he loved the Word and he loved us and wanted us to experience the same life-changing relationship with God's Word that he had experienced.

This was the time in my life God's Word started to become food for my soul. It became a fountain of life for my spiritual walk. While we studied several books in the Bible together during those years, it was our in-depth study of Psalm 119 that really seemed to be what Joe focused on the most. Some of the passages that have continued to echo in my heart and mind are:

- *V. 11*: "Thy word have I hid in mine heart, that I might not sin against thee" (KJV).

- *V. 27*: "Make me to understand the way of thy precepts: so shall I talk of thy wondrous works" (KJV).

- *V. 105*: "Thy word is a lamp unto my feet, and a light unto my path" (KJV).

The lessons I learned from that study fully remain in my heart and memory until this day. Born from that season was a yearning and striving to worship the Father in a manner consistent with the greatest commandment. This is the season I truly learned how to love God's Word. This changed everything for me. My hope is for this book to serve as the catalyst for something similar in your heart as well. Take it slow, don't be in a hurry, and let God's Word do its work in your heart, as it did in mine.

Dr. Samkon Gado
Otolaryngology Resident
St Louis University Hospital
Retired NFL player

Foreword by
Dr. Joshua L. Linebaugh, MD

I will always remember Joe showing up for our weekly Tuesday morning breakfast and accountability sessions my freshman year of high school. For me, the meetings were more about the breakfast buffet than the accountability. Young Pastor Joe was excitable, but that morning was different. Joe's eyes indicated he had a secret to tell me. I was confident he was going to tell me that he met *the one*. That he was finally in love. As breakfast unfolded, it wasn't about meeting his future wife but about his new Bible study on Psalm 119 and his encounter with *the One*. Little did I know that both of our lives would change that day.

In 1995, Joe was my third youth pastor in three years at Three Rivers Baptist Church. I grew up in the church, my family being charter members. I was the favored son, or golden child, in the youth group. I always looked the part and had all the right answers. I walked with arrogance believing the hype. Joe established a discipleship ministry where adult mentors invested in the youth with the goal that those youth would, in turn, mentor the younger kids in our church. To me it made sense that the new youth pastor would pick me to mentor, but what I initially thought was being *picked* turned out to be *targeted.*

Joe recognized my high opinion of myself and targeted me to invest his life to change mine. After building a relationship and developing trust, Joe challenged me. "Josh, I know you think you're the leader of this youth group. I agree you're the social leader, but you aren't the spiritual leader." Talk about audacity. Talk about shock. I am not sure if the shock was more because someone had told me that I was not *the man* or because someone had seen through my façade. Either way, Joe's boldness and insight won my respect and my heart. I was then his to teach.

Shortly after that encounter came the introduction of Psalm 119. Verses like Psalm 119:9 permeated my thoughts and speech: "How can a young man keep his way pure? By guarding it according to your word." Verse 11 was equally impactful: "I have stored up your word in my heart, that I might not sin against you." I spent the entirety of my time in high school studying, journaling, memorizing, and teaching Psalm 119. These words became my closest friends, where I went when being everyone's golden child became too much. I would turn to His promise of forgiveness when my heart wandered. I found comfort knowing when my struggles and sinfulness began to manifest themselves, I could dive back in to Psalm 119, finding comfort in failure.

Turn the page to today—I still struggle with playing the role that everyone wants me to play. I have a wonderful wife and three beautiful kids. I am an emergency medicine physician in the upstate of South Carolina. The world sees success, but my story is filled with many ups and downs. I have struggled with sins, both hidden and visible, and suffered the consequences.

Then I look back to the words of my youth that encouraged and motivated me to seek God with my whole heart, to delight in Him, to meditate on His precepts, and to fix my eyes on His ways (vv. 15–16). This is why I am so excited for each person who reads this book. I am excited that you will be challenged and transformed by God's Word and the wisdom and insights Joe shared with me over breakfast twenty-five-plus years ago. My prayer is that you delight in God's Word and challenge yourself to seek Him with your whole heart.

Dr. Joshua L Linebaugh, MD
D.O., M.B.A., FACOEP

INTRODUCTION

Knowing Him Better

When our family first moved to New York City, I thought I knew what good pizza was. After all, I'd eaten a lot of pizza in my time. Then, a new friend took me to  Lombardi's, the first pizzeria established in the United States, located in the Little Italy neighborhood of Manhattan.

As we walked inside, my friend told me he was going to buy me some pizza.

"Great!" I replied. "I like pizza."

He shook his head. "No, you don't understand. I'm buying you pizza that will change your life."

And, man, was he right! That first slice at Lombardi's was a revelation. Before then, I hadn't really been eating pizza—I had just been eating bread with sauce and cheese on it. I had been unknowingly filling my stomach with a cheap imitation of the original, thinking I was satisfied. I had no idea how amazing pizza could be!

After that, there was no going back. I'll still eat other pizza—if you can call it that—if it's put in front of me, but absolutely nothing can compare to Lombardi's.

I have to confess, there was a time when my relationship with God was like my pre-Lombardi's relationship with pizza. I'm sure you can relate. We read our Bibles, pray a little, and go through the motions of church, completely unaware that there's something amazing waiting for us.

The embarrassing thing is this described my relationship with Heavenly Dad, as I like to call Him, when I was working as a youth pastor. I thought I was doing so well, but I had a shallow understanding of who God is, and I was quite content to stay that way.

All that changed for me when I spent some serious time reading, studying, and meditating on Psalm 119. I kept a journal of my thoughts as I went through this journey all those years ago. In this book, I will share with you what I learned, and even what I wrote in my journal along the way, so that you too can upgrade your relationship with God from frozen-grocery-store-pizza mode to the real deal.

Although there's some debate over who wrote this psalm, I believe it was written by David and, as we study it, I'll tell you why. As you read through this book, understanding the authorship is foundational to some of what we learn, and therefore, we can appreciate the message even more.

Psalm 119 is the longest chapter in the Bible, and it's entirely focused on loving God's Word. Though it can be repetitive, that repetition creates a fantastic musical rhythm that helps make the concepts more memorable. The author of this psalm wrote it to be a symphony of sorts, celebrating and exploring God's Word from many angles.

As we dig deeper into Psalm 119, we'll see it's really a guide, a key, to developing a heart for God and His Word. In 171 out of the psalm's 176 verses, Scripture is referred to by a variety of words: "your laws, judgments, precepts, and commandments," "your ways," and "your path." If you let it, Psalm 119 can serve as an instruction manual for how to have the right attitude and the right heart toward God's Word.

Studying Psalm 119 transformed my life, as you'll see. It was like God opened my heart and performed open heart surgery on me. I saw that I'd been basing my relationship with Him on my selfish desires. I was so focused on what God was doing for me that I completely forgot to look at who God is and what He wants for my life.

Acknowledging what God has done in our lives is not necessarily wrong. It's a problem, however, when the foundation for our relationship with God becomes the work He has done in our hearts and lives rather than who He is. It's human nature to make even our connection to God about us, what we receive, how we feel, or what we believe we need from God. When we understand who God truly is, then we desire to know Him better.

Here's what you'll learn over the course of our study of Psalm 119:

- You'll learn how to be a real worshiper of God. In our modern times, worship tends to be synonymous with a touchy-feely, emotional experience that's enhanced by the quality of the music, lighting, and other effects. We'll be getting back to the roots of what it truly means to worship God.

- You'll learn how to really love God's Word. Too often, we experience Scripture in soundbites—a verse shared on social media, for example. By studying a portion of the Bible in detail and unpacking what it means, you'll develop a greater appreciation for the richness of Scripture and a deeper awe and reverence for our God who inspired it.

- You'll learn how to spend quality, effective, transformational time with God on a more frequent basis. I'll be sharing personal, vulnerable details about how studying Psalm 119 changed my heart, my mind, and my relationship with Heavenly Dad and His Word. My hope is that you'll learn from my experience and maybe avoid some of my struggles.

This book will take you out of your comfort zone and require you to address some hard truths. You will need to truly meditate on Scripture and allow the Holy Spirit to change your perspective.

Are you ready to move past inadequate, impaired, and misguided worship? Are you ready to be in love with God's Word, pursuing its meaning through diligent inquiry? Are you ready to be guided and directed by what you learn through that diligent inquiry? Do you want to see transformation in your life?

Then let's begin! Psalm 119 is divided into twenty-two stanzas of eight verses each. Each stanza is named after a letter in the Hebrew alphabet. By the way, in Hebrew, the words at the end of each line rhyme because Psalm 119 is a poem. Our first chapter will focus on the stanza titled "Aleph."

CHAPTER ONE

Aleph—Diligent Worship

I have to admit that I have very rarely in my life committed to seek God with my whole heart. I confuse emotional experience for commitment to God. How can I pretend to be so committed, so emotional, over something that isn't even a big part of my daily schedule? As I study Psalm 119, I will pray specifically that God gives me a supernatural desire to worship Him through diligent inquiry into His Word so I can actually get to know who I am worshiping.

—From Joe's journal

When I wrote this journal entry, I was chasing those moments where I felt close to God. Sometimes it was a song, sometimes a beautiful mountain. After reading the first eight verses of Psalm 119, I realized I knew more about the song and the mountain than I did about the One who made those things.

My worship was a joke. I wasn't an accountant or a lawyer—I was a pastor! And I felt like I shouldn't be in that role.

One of the biggest obstacles to having a vibrant

relationship with Heavenly Dad is shame due to biblical ignorance. This shame is born out of places in our lives that don't measure up to Scripture because we don't know what God's Word says—or because we know what God's Word says, but we don't want to admit we don't measure up. We may also feel that since we haven't studied those parts of Scripture yet, we don't have to deal with those areas of our lives right now.

This happens when our exposure to God's Word isn't the dominant, guiding priority in our life decisions. We may know part of God's Word, but we don't spend a lot of time in Scripture. As a result, its effects begin to wane.

Historical: Hebrew Word Study

Aleph is the first letter of the Hebrew alphabet. It's also the number one. The first thing the author of Psalm 119 addresses is what obstructs true transformational worship. This is an essential first step in understanding how important God's Word is in our lives.

> *Blessed are the **undefiled** in the way, who walk in the law of the Lord! **Blessed** are those who **keep** His testimonies, who **seek** Him with the whole heart! They also do no iniquity; they walk in His ways. You have commanded us to keep Your precepts diligently. Oh, that my ways were directed to keep Your statutes! Then I would not be **ashamed**, when I look into all Your commandments. I will praise You with uprightness of heart, when I learn Your righteous judgments. I will keep Your statutes; oh, do not forsake me utterly!*
> —***Psalm 119:1–8*** (NKJV, emphasis added)

Let's look closer at some words in the passage above.

The Hebrew word for undefiled (v. 1) is *tamim*, which means "without blemish, complete, full, perfect, sincere."[1] In this passage, the word focuses on sincerity. Blessed are those who are sincere.

In verse 2, the word translated as "blessed" is the Hebrew word *asre*. It's constructed as an interjection and refers to fulfillment, so we could read this phrase as "how fulfilled!"[2] Do you ever feel your worship should be more fulfilling than it is? Sometimes we even fake it, raising our hands and swaying in hopes of getting into the worship experience. But this verse tells us that fulfillment doesn't come from the experience. It teaches us that fulfillment comes from diligently seeking to know the character and qualities of God that make him worthy of our worship. Let's do a deeper dive into some key words in verse 2 that help make this clear.

The word "keep" in verse 2 is the Hebrew word *natsar*, which means "to protect, maintain, obey, observe, or preserve." To protect something, you need to stay close to it.[3] We can't keep God's testimonies if we're not consistently spending time with His Word. To be effective in spending time in God's Word, we need to protect our time in it and not allow life's distractions to hinder us. We might fake a worship experience, but there is no faking spending time in the Bible.

Also in verse 2, the word translated as "seek" is the Hebrew word *darash*, meaning "to seek or inquire."[4] We are to worship God because of diligent inquiry into His Word, taking the time, effort, and energy to really understand what it's saying, and why, how, and to whom.

The last word we'll examine in this passage is "ashamed" (v. 6), which is the Hebrew word *bos*. In this context, this word conveys disappointment, a sense that something is delayed or has become dry.[5] Disappointment is when your worship is like cotton candy; it tasted good, but it's already gone. The emotional experience is over so quickly that you feel guilty about not having that feeling anymore. It's unfulfilling, and you're still hungry and unsatisfied.

Theological: Eradicating Shame Through Diligent Inquiry

If we're really going to understand what worship is about, we need to get rid of that mentality and eliminate the shame that comes from ignorance regarding what God's Word says about our lives.

> *Oh, that my ways were directed to keep Your statutes!*
> *Then I would not be ashamed, when I look into all Your*
> *commandments.*
> **—Psalm 119:5–6** *(NKJV)*

In other words, the psalmist wished his ways were forced to keep God's statutes. Then he would not be ashamed when he read God's Word.

When Scripture is not a frequent presence in our lives, we experience this shame that is a barrier to our worship of God. It's a result of a lack of diligent inquiry into God's Word.

This is my journal entry from the second day of my study of Psalm 119, well over two decades ago. I must admit, I was ashamed as I re-read these words:

> *My worship of God is such a joke. It's surface-y. It's*
> *showy. It's a mile wide and an inch deep. It troubles me*
> *so much that I do not know where to begin, except by*
> *simply making two efforts: 1) I long to not be ashamed,*
> *and 2) I long to know what to worship about God and*
> *why. I want to know why it should be so fulfilling. I want*
> *to know more about Him, who He is, not just what He*
> *has done. To do this, I must have significantly more*

*exposure to God's Word. I want to know why He's so
great.*

—*From Joe's journal*

At that time, I was so overcome with disappointment
in who I was—not just as a pastor but as a Christian, as a
man—because I was struck with the stark realization that
I did not worship God through diligent inquiry into His
Word. I worshiped Him through the cotton candy of emotional experience.

*To do this, I must engage in diligent inquiry. This will be
a tough journey, with moments of failure. But hey, that's
what grace is for, right? The important thing for me isn't
perfection but direction.*

—*From Joe's journal*

That last part is very important. These journal entries
show you my state of mind as I studied Psalm 119. As a
young man in his mid-twenties, I was not a very good
Christian—and I was getting paid to be one!

I want you to feel exposed and inadequate, but I don't
want you to feel guilty. The key to this journey is direction, not perfection. I hope you can relate to what I'm
sharing because we will never be perfect in this life. However, our direction is to continue growing closer to God.

Following the psalmist's mention of shame (v. 6), he
then explained that because he learned God's righteous
judgments—that is, because he inquired diligently into
Scripture—he was able to praise God with uprightness of
heart. In other words, he was able to praise God with confidence.

*I will **praise** You with uprightness of heart, when I learn Your righteous judgments. I will keep Your statutes; oh, do not forsake me utterly!*
—**Psalm 119:7–8** *(NKJV, emphasis added)*

Likewise, when we worship God through diligent inquiry into Scripture, when we learn about His judgments, His truth, His law, and His Word, we can worship Him confidently and with upright hearts. Why? Because we then have a better understanding of who we are worshiping and why. We will have been freed from the burden of tying the depth of our worship to how strongly our emotions are affected.

Defining the Target of Your Worship

When I dug a little deeper into the word "praise" in verse 7, what I learned just blew me away. The Hebrew word used is *yadah*, which means to physically throw a stone or shoot an arrow at a target or away from a specific spot, or to make a specific confession.[6]

The psalmist used this very specific archery term to describe praise. He literally shot his worship at a particular target, like an archer shooting an arrow.

You can only do that when you have a defined target. Otherwise, it would be like someone giving you a bow and arrow and telling you just to shoot it wherever. That's not going to end well!

Many times, that's exactly what our worship is like. We're told to praise and worship God, but we're not given enough knowledge and information about His Word to know what to shoot our praise at. Our worship should be aimed, directed, and shot forth—not just thrown out there in hopes that it'll stick.

Imagine an Olympic archer being judged not on the

accuracy of the shot but on how beautiful the shot looked: "Man, that is an incredible shot! That arrow is beautifully crafted and perfectly balanced; the point is sharp, and the feathers are fine. It flies through the air so smoothly, so effortlessly, aimed at nothing in particular."

The archer who wins the gold medal is praised for the perfect flight of the arrow, despite the fact it landed in the stands rather than hitting the target. But that's okay because it was a beautiful shot!

Do you see how praise as defined in this passage is dependent on your worship having a specific target? Can you see how not having a target can cause problems in worship? And can you see that you cannot have a specific target without first learning Scripture through diligent inquiry?

All over the world, we have churches that worship without a target. Worshiping God without understanding His Word is like chasing a spiritual carrot that's always out of reach. You might get close enough to smell it, you might even get close enough that it swings back and bops you on the head, but you never quite get to eat it.

Worship without diligent inquiry is seeking to fulfill our appetite for connection with God without being willing to cook the meal first. We depend on a song, a relationship, lighting, staging, or production to produce an experience or emotion we hope will connect us to Heavenly Dad at a deeper level. Do you see how silly that is? Cotton-candy worship tastes good for a moment but does not produce a lasting transformation.

Biblical worship is objective, not subjective. It must always be done for a specific reason. There must be an objective target, and that target is specific and informed.

We Must Continually Learn About God

Psalm 119:1–8 teaches us that to worship God correctly and get that fulfilling experience with Him we crave, we must constantly be learning about Him. This is why we need to be exposed to His Word continually, intellectually, and with discipline.

Our worship must be founded upon diligent inquiry into Scripture, not experience-chasing, no matter how real that experience may feel. The Word of God is what transforms us—not a song, not a stage, and not talented musicians.

Our goal for worship should be this: transformation through diligent inquiry, not emotional experience. Emotions can be a welcome by-product of hitting that target, but they should not be our focus.

As an example, the Easter Sunday service at the church I pastor was about resurrection and redemption. Our worship team sang and played with those themes as their target, and we experienced emotions as a by-product of them hitting that target. I saw it on people's faces; it was transformational.

This was not because of the skill and talent of our musicians and singers—though we do have an amazing worship team—but because we were hitting the target through diligent inquiry. We made a decision as a team that we wanted to remind the congregation about resurrection and redemption, and our worship director took the time to examine the Scriptures for the sermon and read my notes and choose songs that would hit that target.

The target isn't determined by how good the music will sound but by what we are learning through our diligent inquiry into Scripture.

Devotional: It's Time to Get Uncomfortable

Over the next several chapters, I will attempt to inspire and equip you for your worship through diligent inquiry. From the first stanza of Psalm 119, we know true worship begins with diligent inquiry into God's Word and that will never happen unless we first fall in love with His Word. My study of Psalm 119 did not make me comfortable. More than once, I wanted to quit and study something more comfortable for me, like Philippians, but I stuck with it until the end. This study will make you feel vulnerable and wrecked, and you'll come away from it thinking about changes you need to make. The goal is to help you examine your heart, see what is broken, and heal it.

We will learn what it means to worship God, not by chasing an experience but through diligent inquiry into the power, the dynamo, and the genesis of transformation that is the Word of God.

WORKBOOK

Chapter One Questions

Question: How would you describe your worship? Is it deep or shallow? Is it based on emotions or realities? Is it based on what God has done for you or who God is? Are there areas of your life where you feel ashamed for not following the truths of God's Word?

_____

_____

_____

_____

_____

_____

_____

_____

_____

_____

Question: Keep in mind *direction, not perfection.* How can the pursuit of perfection become counterproductive? What is the role of grace in worship? Read Romans 8:1. How does God graciously direct us?

_____

_____

_____

_____

_____

_____

_____

_____

_____

_____

Question: If your worship times were arrows, would they be hitting a target or shot out at random? Contrast worship that is focused with worship that is unfocused. When have you experienced both in your life? How will you move from aimless to focused worship?

_____

_____

_____

_____

_____

_____

_____

_____

_____

_____

_____

Action: As you begin this study, write out your commitment to diligently seek and study God's Word in order to learn more about who He is and to experience the true worship that He longs for you to enjoy. Place your commitment in your Bible or where you will see it often to remind you to be faithful even when you feel uncomfortable and challenged by the transforming truths of Psalm 119.

_____

_____

_____

_____

_____

_____

_____

_____

Chapter One Notes

CHAPTER TWO

Beth—Sober Wisdom

The first time I noticed myself transitioning from a spiritual child to a wise adult was when I was a young pastor. I was in a leadership meeting with about thirty other men—elders, deacons, other pastors. I was by far the youngest, at least ten years younger than the next oldest, and most were much older. We were talking about how as leaders in the church, we become better at our time in God's Word. This was about a month and a half into me studying Psalm 119 every day. I was just sitting quietly, but Psalm 119 had really been rocking my heart. Then one of the pastors, Tom, says, "I've watched Pastor Joe over the last six to seven weeks turn into an expert on how to love God's Word. Tell them what you taught me about Psalm 119." My jaw dropped! I stood up and shared the precious concepts that I had learned. "With my lips I have declared All the judgments of Your mouth" (v. 13 NKJV)—that was happening to me right there at that moment. As I spoke, I sensed for the first time that I was loving what I was talking about. I couldn't talk enough about it. I realized that, 'I have rejoiced in the way of Your testimonies, As much as in all riches' (v. 14 NKJV). I was having more fun doing that than I could ever have on a cruise ship! It sounds nuts, but it's true.

It was at that moment my mind rushed back to the first journal entry I shared with you earlier. How can I be a pastor? Because God's Word was transforming me, growing me, changing me, replacing fleshly desires with sober wisdom.

The first two verses of the second stanza of Psalm 119, titled "Beth," capture the process and explain the meaning of the rest of the verses in this stanza:

> *How can a young man cleanse his way? By taking heed according to Your word. With my whole heart I have sought You; oh, let me not wander from Your commandments!*
> —***Psalm 119:9–10*** *(NKJV)*

This stanza starts with a question from the perspective of a young man. It then concludes with a description of that young man who has been transformed by spending time with God's Word. The answer to the question he posed—how a young man can cleanse his way—is given by a wise, older man who was once a young man.

> *I am moved by the phrase, 'How can a young man cleanse his way' (v.9). Just three days in, Psalm 119 has vastly increased my awareness of my lack of wisdom and holiness. If people knew what I know now, they would never let me be a pastor.*
> —***From Joe's journal***

It seems funny looking back, but when I wrote it, I was distraught. I was beside myself, wondering, *"What am I doing here?"* I was only three days into my study of Psalm 119, and it had already brought me to a place emotionally, mentally, and spiritually where I recognized that I was ashamed. I was a young man who needed his way cleansed.

Historical: Hebrew Word Study

Let's take a closer look at a few of the words in the first two verses of this stanza.

> *How can a young man **cleanse** his way? By **taking heed** according to Your word. With my whole heart I have sought You; oh, let me not **wander** from Your commandments!*
>
> *—Psalm 119:9–10 (NKJV, emphasis added)*

The Hebrew word translated as "cleanse" is *zakah*, which means "to be translucent, innocent, to make clean."[7] It can also mean "transparent," which means that you leave nothing hidden. You put yourself in a place of vulnerability where everything about you can be analyzed and diagnosed.

"Taking heed" is the Hebrew word *shamar*, meaning "to be wise, to live circumspectly."[8] This word indicates that you come to a point where you become aware of dangers.

And lastly, we have the word "wander," which is from the Hebrew word *shagah*. This word paints a picture of a person who has strayed as though intoxicated,[9] stumbling around in a drunken stupor, enraptured by ignorance.

Theological: Supernatural Awareness

The problem highlighted in Psalm 119:9–10 is not

necessarily a literal struggle with alcohol or another substance. That's not the only circumstance that can produce a drunken stupor.

It can also come from your fleshly desires for money, sex, power, or relationships. Any number of things can dominate—your passions, emotions, and decisions—intoxicating you to such a degree that your sole focus is getting more of these things.

The problem here is a foolish, immature lifestyle. To rectify that, you'll need supernatural awareness—an awareness of the things of God. Understanding the satisfying riches of what God has to offer will help you turn away from the emptiness and insatiability of the lusts of the world.

That is why this stanza begins with the question of how a young man can cleanse his way. This is not necessarily someone who is young in age but rather someone who is unwise, inexperienced, and who thinks only of fulfilling their lusts. But it's important to recognize signs of not pursuing things of God.

Signs of Intoxication

How can you tell if you're wandering around in a drunken stupor, pursuing your own lusts instead of the things of God? Let's take a look at what Scripture has to say.

The first sign of intoxication is being asleep—not necessarily physically but spiritually, intellectually, emotionally. You are unaware of what's going on around you, "So then let us not sleep, as others do, but let us keep awake and be sober" (1 Thessalonians 5:6).

The second sign of intoxication is the continual pursuit of pleasure, "But watch yourselves lest your hearts be weighed down with dissipation and drunkenness and cares of this life, and that day come upon you suddenly like a trap" (Luke 21:34). That's tied to the shame we talked about in the previous chapter. Someone who is intoxicated, wandering around in a drunken stupor, is driven by their desires and constantly looking to fulfill them. They'll do whatever is necessary to gratify their lusts. They are asleep and unaware of the consequences of their actions because they are only focused on pleasing themselves.

As people of faith, we are called to be spiritually awake and sober:

Therefore, preparing your minds for action, and being sober-minded, set your hope fully on the grace that will be brought to you at the revelation of Jesus Christ.
—1 Peter 1:13

Be sober-minded; be watchful. Your adversary the devil prowls around like a roaring lion, seeking someone to devour.
—1 Peter 5:8

When someone is stumbling around in a drunken stupor, they can't see the dangers around them as they're fulfilling the lusts of their flesh. They are so hell-bent on satisfying their desires that they can't see the consequences standing right at the gate, ready to devour them.

"How can a young man cleanse his way?" (Psalm 119:9 NKJV) becomes the heart cry of anyone who is desperately longing for God. Holiness and sobriety become burning issues. As we enter a new stage of spiritual growth, God's Word gives us an acute awareness of our lack of sobriety and holiness and our desperate need for sober wisdom.

Once you see that your way, your life, needs cleansing,

the Word of God miraculously implants in you an earnest craving for a remedy.

Sobering Up

> Your word I have hidden in my heart, that I might not sin against You. Blessed are You, O Lord! Teach me Your statutes. With my lips I have declared all the judgments of Your mouth. I have rejoiced in the way of Your testimonies, as much as in all riches. I will meditate on Your precepts, and contemplate Your ways. I will delight myself in Your statutes; I will not forget Your word.
>
> **—Psalm 119:11–16 (NKJV)**

The first proof that God's Word is performing open-heart surgery in your life is a life-rocking sense of your lack of sobriety in your actions, words, relationships, and decisions.

The second proof is there is a sudden transition to sober wisdom. This may happen without you even realizing it. We begin to crave this transition from immaturity and spiritually intoxicated living, dominated by the desire to fulfill our flesh, to maturity and a life marked by sober wisdom and all that comes with it. Our words and actions miraculously come into line with God's Word.

> But that is not the way you learned Christ!—assuming that you have heard about him and were taught in him, as the truth is in Jesus, to put off your old self, which belongs to your former manner of life and is corrupt through deceitful desires, and to be renewed in the spirit of your minds, and to put on the new self, created after the likeness of God in true righteousness and holiness.
>
> **—Ephesians 4:20–24**

This passage describes someone transitioning from spiritually intoxicated living to a place of sober wisdom and maturity. Psalm 119:11–16 takes it a step further, providing signs you are entering a place of sober wisdom. Which of these signs are you seeing in your life?

- You make better decisions—financially, relationally, schedule-wise, career-wise, etc. "Your word I have hidden in my heart, that I might not sin against You" (v. 11 NKJV).

- Your speech becomes godlier and more gracious. "With my lips I have declared all the judgments of Your mouth" (v. 13 NKJV).

- Your personal values change, prioritizing the Word of God above all else. "I have rejoiced in the way of Your testimonies, as much as in all riches" (v. 14 NKJV). It's impossible to think of God's Word as more important than money unless you are entering a stage of sober wisdom.

- Your thought process changes. When you think through things, God's concepts and truths come into your mind, and you use those to analyze and make decisions. "I will meditate on Your precepts, and contemplate Your ways" (v. 15 NKJV). Meditating, in this sense, doesn't mean sitting with your legs crossed and saying, "Om." It means to muse, consider, think about, and ponder God's Word. The psalmist is not talking about his physical eyes in this verse but about his spiritual eyes, his goal, and his direction.

- Your delights change. "I will delight myself in Your statutes; I will not forget Your word" (v.

16 NKJV). The things you enjoy begin to change. It becomes easier to follow Jesus as you spend more time in Scripture because the things your flesh used to love will become less important than the new things you crave.

As you spend time in God's Word and move from wandering around in a drunken stupor to a place of sober wisdom, your fleshly desires fade. The things you used to think were so important pale in comparison to Christian fellowship, spending time in God's Word, celebrating God, worshiping Him, and seeing other people's lives transformed.

If you're in a drunken stupor, you don't care when other people sober up and become wise—all you're thinking about is getting what you want. But when wisdom enters your life, you delight in the things of God, and they begin to replace your fleshly desires.

This Book of the Law shall not depart from your mouth, but you shall meditate in it day and night, that you may observe to do according to all that is written in it. For then you will make your way prosperous, and then you will have good success.
—Joshua 1:8 (NKJV)

Think about this amazing transition for a moment. Taking time for diligent inquiry into Scripture makes you sober and vigilant, transforming you from a silly, foolish, drunkenly wandering child enslaved to the desires of your flesh to a person with sober wisdom.

Remember the story I shared at the beginning of this chapter? As others witness this miraculous transformation, you inevitably become a resource to them. It's not that you're seeking to declare what you've learned; it just happens naturally, without you even thinking about it. Having these organic opportunities to share what you're learning with others is one sign you're falling in love with God's Word.

It's not the physical book that performs this miracle—the binding and the pages. Yet as Christians, we sometimes make the mistake of venerating the book itself. The physical book is not holy or righteous; it simply contains holy and righteous concepts.

This transformation is the result of the words in those pages, coupled with the power of the Holy Spirit through the gift of faith. These words gave me sober wisdom that helped me to begin to put away the childish lusts of my flesh.

As I mentioned in the journal entry at the beginning of this chapter, men older and better than me found this wisdom valuable enough that they wanted to emulate it! It was so humbling and so encouraging. That day, my love for the power of God's Word in my life was solidified forever.

I thought, "I'm going to 'meditate on Your precepts, and contemplate Your ways. I will delight myself in Your statutes; I will not forget Your word.' (vv. 15–16 NKJV)—*because I've just seen what it did for me over the last two to three months. Where I am right now, I know where I'm going. I know what's important to me: Your Word.*"

I finally understood what the psalmist was saying. Everything came together and clicked; the light came on. This was the moment of the reality of God's Word in my life, and it gave me the resolve to alter the course of my relationship with Heavenly Dad for the rest of my days.

I recognized my relationship with God is not based on my Sunday school attendance, how good my sermons are, or the size of the congregation I pastor. It's based on how much I pursue Him in His Word, in His truth.

Devotional: A New Addiction

I want so desperately for each of you to experience that humbling yet empowering moment I had that day. I want Psalm 119 to inspire that leap of faith in God's Word, to transform your hearts and your lives.

I want you to see how Heavenly Dad will step up when that "let me not wander from Your commandments" (v. 10 NKJV) moment happens, that moment when you say, "I don't want to stray from Your Word anymore. I don't want to be that person wandering around in a drunken stupor any longer." I want you to see how He will help you understand and use the people around you who no longer wander, just as He did for the author of Psalm 119.

The psalmist was a young man who needed his way cleansed, and he fell in love with God's Word. He wrote this incredible, twenty-two stanza, "Stairway to Heaven"-length song about how much the Word of God transformed his life. When I started studying it, it transformed my life too, taking me from a young pastor wandering in a drunken stupor to a person who, with brokenness and humility, began to experience all the benefits of sober wisdom.

Every time God's Word does something in your heart, you experience the benefits, and it drives you right back to His Word. You won't be able to get enough! Instead of being addicted to the desires of your flesh, you'll be addicted to the truth that transforms your heart and life.

WORKBOOK

Chapter Two Questions

Question: What thing(s) have intoxicated your soul—
whether an actual substance or a fleshly desire for pleasure of some type that drives your life and dulls your
spiritual senses? Why is this intoxication ultimately insa-
tiable and empty? How has it made you asleep to your
own and others' spiritual condition?

_____

_____

_____

_____

_____

_____

_____

_____

_____

_____

_____

_____

Question: Describe a believer you know who is walking in sober wisdom. How is it evident in their life? How do you see a pursuit of God's Word manifested in this believer's life and what have you learned from them?

_____

_____

_____

_____

_____

_____

_____

_____

_____

_____

_____

Question: How would your life be different if you were addicted to God's Word instead of empty and fleshly pursuits? For example, how might walking in scriptural sober wisdom begin to change your relationships, your job, your dreams and goals, your free time, your health choices, and your finances?

_____

_____

_____

_____

_____

_____

_____

_____

_____

_____

Action: Sincerely ask God to use His Word to perform open-heart surgery in your life. Then commit yourself to His Word. How often will you read it, and what will be your reading plan? How and what portion will you study in depth? What passage will you memorize or "hide in your heart" as the psalmist says?

_____

_____

_____

_____

_____

_____

_____

_____

_____

Chapter Two Notes

CHAPTER THREE

Gimel—Separation

The third stanza of Psalm 119, titled "Gimel," is a conclusion to the second stanza. It answers the question, "How can a young man cleanse his way? By taking heed according to Your Word" (Psalm 119:9 NKJV), as the psalmist continues to develop this theme of moving from immaturity to maturity.

It's good in theory to break our bondage to sin, but we need a concrete first step to break out of the prison of loving the world more than God.

This passage explains the first step to living with sober wisdom is separation—being weaned off the desires we're addicted to and the lust that causes us to pursue these desires as though we are in a drunken stupor.

I never realized how immature and arrogant my Bible reading is. I expect to see things that others can't see, that I am smart enough to uncover wondrous things with my own eyes and mind. I never realized how immature and helpless I am to see things without God revealing them to me. I need God's perspective of His Word, not mine. Starting today, I will beg God to "open my eyes" when reading His Word.

And that's exactly what God did in my heart as I studied these first three verses.

Historical: Hebrew Word Study

The poetic imagery in these verses is just beautiful. The psalmist sets forth three images of separation, and then, at the end of the stanza, there's an image of joining.

> **Deal bountifully** with Your servant, that I may live and keep Your word. Open my eyes, that I may see **wondrous** things from Your law. I am a **stranger** in the earth; do not **hide** Your commandments from me.
> **—Psalm 119:17–19** (NKJV, emphasis added)

1. The first image of separation is separation from immaturity. The Hebrew word translated as "deal bountifully" is *gamal,* but that English translation doesn't quite capture what the psalmist is communicating within the context of the psalm.[10]

Since this stanza is a response to the question "How can a young man cleanse his way?" (v. 9 NKJV)—that is, how can someone spiritually immature develop sober wisdom—the psalmist is using the word *gamal* in the sense of weaning or ripening, of completing a child's nursing.[11] He asks God to wean him off his love for this world. What an incredible connection to the previous stanza!

The psalmist begged God to reward his pursuit by maturing him and then by separating him from his fleshly desires and the world he adores. In an act of supernatural humility, as he read Scripture he thought of himself as a child who needed to be weaned.

Why did the psalmist want to be weaned off childishness and ripened into spiritual maturity? So he could keep God's Word and live together with it. But how did he believe this would happen?

2. *That brings us to the second image of separation, which is separation in the Word.* The Hebrew word translated as "wondrous" is *pala*, which indicates something is distinguished or marvelous.[12] The psalmist asked God to separate out wonderful things from His Word as he read it, things other people were not able to see.

This goes beyond asking for mere understanding—he wanted to see the distinguished, marvelous things God has hidden in His Word, the *wow things.* He asked God to separate him from the world by separating out the wondrous things from God's Word. The psalmist desired to be mature, to stop eating like a baby and start eating like an adult. We see this concept in a passage from Hebrews.

> *For though by this time you ought to be teachers, you need someone to teach you again the basic principles of the oracles of God. You need milk, not solid food, for everyone who lives on milk is unskilled in the word of righteousness, since he is a child. But solid food is for the mature, for those who have their powers of discernment trained by constant practice to distinguish good from evil.*
> **—Hebrews 5:12–14**

Do you see what's happening here? The psalmist asked God to wean him so he would be able to keep God's law. The author of Hebrews also wants his readers to eat meat so he could practice it and know what God's law is, what is good and what is evil.

3. *The third image of separation is separation from the world.* Here's my journal entry from the very next day:

It amazes me how many things distract me from reading God's Word. I wish my hunger for God's Word was as strong as my appetite for a value meal at lunch. Nothing around me helps me spend time in God's Word, outside of the gift of faith and the supernatural desire to know Him better.

—From Joe's journal

I was recognizing as I read these verses that my world was filled with things that kept me from finding *wow things* in Scripture. This really had an impact on me because I was too caught up in the day-to-day things in this life, allowing them to fill my time. Even if we are going about life and fulfilling our responsibilities, we still need to find time to grow in God's Word.

The word "stranger" in verse 19 of Psalm 119 is the Hebrew word *ger*, which indicates a person who is on a temporary journey or only staying in a place for a certain amount of time.[13] The psalmist considered himself a foreigner, a stranger, in this world because of what God's Word was doing in his life by weaning him off his love of the world and showing him wondrous things that have been separated out from God's Word by the power of God.

The psalmist thought of himself as being in the world because God had things for him to do. He loved eternal things, not the things of this world.

The word "hide," also in verse 19, is the Hebrew word *çathar*, meaning "to hide by covering, to keep close or concealed."[14] Here, the psalmist repeats the theme of seeking understanding he began in verse 18 with the expression, "Open my eyes, that I may see..." (NKJV).

Hebrew often repeats the same thing in a different way for emphasis—for example, "I went to the store to get milk; yes, I drove to 7-Eleven and got dairy products."

So, the first time, the psalmist said, "Open my eyes, that I may behold wondrous things out of your law," and the second time, he said to "hide not your commandments from me." He asked God to reveal things to him that are hidden in His Word, and then he repeated this prayer using different phrasing, asking God not to hide things from him that are hidden by default from those who do not have the gift of faith.

Falling out of Love with the World

> *My soul breaks with longing for Your judgments at all times. You rebuke the proud—the cursed, who stray from Your commandments. Remove from me reproach and contempt, for I have kept Your testimonies. Princes also sit and speak against me, but Your servant meditates on Your statutes. Your testimonies also are my delight and my counselors.*
>
> **—Psalm 119:20–24** *(NKJV)*

The psalmist wanted to separate from the world. He wanted those wow things in Scripture to be so powerful they wean him off his love of the world. He wanted them to be so good, so amazing, so enticing that they make a Ferrari look like a 1980s Hyundai.

He wanted to be separated from how the world lives, thinks, and derives its motives for living. If you're wandering around in a drunken stupor, your motives for living are very different from someone who is walking in sober wisdom, who has had wondrous things revealed to them.

The psalmist wanted God to enhance the gift of faith He had given him, make it stronger, more powerful so he could see things others could not. In verses 20–24, he describes what life in the world is like without God's Word: a drunken wandering filled with scorn and contempt, susceptible to all kinds of traps.

Our tendency is to trust the wrong type of wisdom, the wrong type of counselors. We rely on the wisdom of this world. It's hard to see God's Word from God's perspective through His wisdom when our vision is obstructed by our love of the things around us.

We blame it on *the world*—just as we blame things on the famous *they*—but the primary obstacle getting in the way of seeing wondrous things in Scripture is the world we build around ourselves, our condominiums of sinfulness, our strip malls of sin. We spend so much time building these things—careers, relationships, etc.—we fall in love with them and desperately need to be weaned and separated from them.

How does this process of being weaned and separated happen? It starts with God separating out wondrous things from His Word that make you fall out of love with temporal things and fall in love with eternal things. Just as the Word of God weaned the psalmist off trusting the things he could see and caused him to fall in love with sober wisdom, it will do the same for us if we let it!

Theological: Joining with God's Wisdom

After these three images of separation, the psalmist ends this stanza with an image of joining with the counsel and wisdom of God's Word.

> *Your testimonies also are my delight and my counselors.*
> **—Psalm 119:24** *(NKJV)*

The psalmist now rejects the counsel of the world and embraces the counsel of God. The wow things in God's Word became his sober wisdom.

Being connected to God's sober wisdom gives you the

ability to look at a tempting world, knowing nothing it can offer, nothing anyone can say or do, will keep you from loving God's Word. The Word of God will remain the center of your life regardless of how nice a car you buy. This happens when we recognize the momentary, temporal nature of the world around us—even the worlds we've built, like our comfortable churches, even the façade of perfect families.

However, you won't see how temporary the world is or how valuable eternity is unless God has allowed you to see those wow things first:

> But our citizenship is in heaven, and from it we await a Savior, the Lord Jesus Christ, who will transform our lowly body to be like his glorious body, by the power that enables him even to subject all things to himself.
> —**Philippians 3:20–21**

The drunken stupor of worldliness prevents you from seeing the wondrous things in God's Word: "Beloved, I urge you as sojourners and exiles to abstain from the passions of the flesh, which wage war against your soul" (1 Peter 2:11).

Once your heart begins to wean off its love of the world and turns to the wow things in Scripture, you start to seek those treasures that are eternal instead of temporal:

> Do not lay up for yourselves treasures on earth, where moth and rust destroy and where thieves break in and steal, but lay up for yourselves treasures in heaven, where neither moth nor rust destroys and where thieves do not break in and steal. For where your treasure is, there your heart will be also.
> —**Matthew 6:19–21**

For this light momentary affliction is preparing for us an eternal weight of glory beyond all comparison, as we look not to the things that are seen but to the things that are unseen. For the things that are seen are transient, but the things that are unseen are eternal.

—2 Corinthians 4:17–18

Devotional: We Need To Ask God

Can you see how supernatural intervention is necessary for us to stop trusting things you can touch, feel and begin to trust in eternal things? As the author of Hebrews wrote, "Now faith is the assurance of things hoped for, the conviction of things not seen" (Hebrews 11:1).

Time in God's Word causes our love of temporary things to fade as passion for God's wow things crowds out the allure of temporal, worldly possessions, counsel, and wisdom. This will be outwardly evident to those around you through your decisions, relationships, and sober wisdom.

I'm not saying you'll be perfect, never again struggling with sin—I want to relieve you of that burden. But as God's wow things wean you off your love of the world, there will be an unmistakable direction. As He separates out wondrous things from His law for you, you will naturally begin to separate from the world around you. Soon, the only thing that will satisfy you are those wow things God separates out and reveals to you.

So how can we start the weaning process? It very simple, by praying the short prayer in the first verse of the stanza: "Deal bountifully with Your servant, that I may live and keep Your word. Open my eyes, that I may behold wondrous things out of your law" (Psalm 119:17–18).

Wean me off the world and open my eyes to wow things. Yes it's a simple idea, but it takes supernatural intervention to find things so wondrous that they wean you off your love of this world. This won't be something you accomplish simply with discipline alone. Discipline is not where the power of spiritual transformation lies. In fact, any discipline will be the result of God answering this prayer. The power of being weaned off your love of the world will be the wow things in Scripture that God opens your eyes to see—so much so that the last verse of this stanza is as true of you as it was of the psalmist: "Your testimonies also are my delight and my counselors" (Psalm 119:24 NKJV).

This describes a complete 180! He has been weaned off the things of this world, and he now loves the things of eternity.

It's supernatural, so for this to happen we need to ask God to do this for us every day. You want to be weaned off your love of the temporal world around you, even the ones you have built yourself? Even your comfy religion? Then I challenge you to pray these twelve words daily: "Wean me off the world and open my eyes to wow things."

Are you so distracted by the world around you that you can't make a three-second commitment to ask God to wean you off it? If so, that is proof you're in love with the temporary world and desperately need to be weaned from it.

I'm asking you to trust me on this. Starting today, and each day after, ask God to wean you off the world and open your eyes to wow things in His word. It won't be long before you begin to see things change!

WORKBOOK

Chapter Three Questions

Question: Do you consider yourself a mature *meat-eating* believer whom others could follow as an example, or are you still drinking *milk*? What indicators of Christian maturity or of spiritual immaturity are in your life? Are your insights from God's Word deep, personal, and powerful, or are they shallow and learned from others?

_____

_____

_____

_____

_____

_____

_____

_____

_____

Question: What are some things about which you are enthusiastic and feel a sense of awe? The psalmist asked God to separate him from the world by separating out the wondrous things from God's Word. Describe a time when you said "wow" over God's Word. What led to you seeing these wondrous things? Are such moments a regular part of your time with the Lord?

_____

_____

_____

_____

_____

_____

_____

_____

_____

_____

Question: Read James 3:13–18. Contrast the wisdom of this world vs. the wisdom of God. Give examples of each kind of wisdom.

_____

_____

_____

_____

_____

_____

_____

_____

_____

_____

_____

Action: Write out this prayer at the end of the chapter: _Wean me off the world and open my eyes to wow things._ Make it into a bookmark or a sign that you can keep with your Bible, and pray these words each time you open God's Word.

_____

_____

_____

_____

_____

_____

_____

_____

_____

_____

Chapter Three Notes

CHAPTER FOUR

Daleth—What You Cling To

In the previous chapter, I mentioned we aren't expecting perfection when it comes to loving God's Word and weaning off the world; we're looking for unmistakable direction. The psalmist knew from his life there would be times when he would take two steps back, relapsing into his love affair with the world.

This stanza, titled "Daleth," expands on the conflict that exists between the love of God's Word and the love of the world. It teaches us that clinging to this world is like clinging to dirt and then shows us the miracle of how we can thrive even when life is almost too hard to imagine.

This lesson has proven invaluable in my own life, amid devastating loss. More on that later.

Historical: Hebrew Word Study

*My soul clings to the **dust**; revive me according to Your word. I have declared my ways, and You answered me; teach me Your statutes. Make me understand the way of Your precepts; so shall I meditate on Your wonderful works. My soul **melts** from heaviness; strengthen me according to Your word. Remove from me the way of lying,*

and grant me Your law graciously. I have chosen the way
*of truth; Your judgments I have laid before me. I **cling** to*
Your testimonies; O LORD, do not put me to shame! I will
*run the course of Your commandments, for You shall **en-***
***large** my heart.*

—**Psalm 119:25–32** *(NKJV, emphasis added)*

Let's take a closer look at some of the original Hebrew
in these verses. The Hebrew word translated as "dust" in
verse 25 is *aphar,* which means "dust or dry earth—specifically, the material to which the human body returns."[15]
Essentially, the psalmist is saying, "My soul clings to the
very ashes I come from and I will return to."

In verse 28, the word translated as "melts" is the Hebrew *dalaph,* meaning "to drop through, to melt, or to
pour out."[16] The psalmist, who loved God and His Word
and made God's Word a priority in his life, feels like he
was eating dirt—the dirt from his decomposed human
body—and his soul was melting with sorrow.

That doesn't sound like prosperity to me. It sounds like
someone struggling with real life. The psalmist is confessing how he felt when it seemed to him the world started to
win again. His heart was heavy with pressure and stress;
he was in an emotional state of limpness, feeling burned
down.

"Cling" in verse 31 is the Hebrew word *dabaq,* which
expresses the concept of clinging or cleaving to something
as closely as skin does to bone.[17] In contrast to the psalmist clinging to the dust in verse 25, he now clings to God's
testimonies, His Word. Even though the psalmist's soul
had melted and his life had been burned to the ground by
the world around him, whether through his love of the
world or its hatred of him, he clung like skin to the bone
to God's Word and the wow things God had allowed him
to discover.

Lastly, in verse 32, "enlarge" is translated from the

Hebrew *rachab*, which indicates growing wide and thriving, like a broad and roomy pasture.[18] As God widened the psalmist's heart and soul, he went from clinging to the dirt of decomposed human remains to running in wide, roomy pastures.

It's a beautiful picture, and the contrast is striking. When we have a prior relationship with God's Word and we are able to cling to it amidst a life that has been melted to the ground, God will bring us into green pastures.

Theological: Face Down in the Dirt

My soul clings to the dust; revive me according to Your word. I have declared my ways, and You answered me; teach me Your statutes. Make me understand the way of Your precepts; so shall I meditate on Your wonderful works. My soul melts from heaviness; strengthen me according to Your word.

—Psalm 119:25–28 *(NKJV)*

These verses paint a vivid picture of the psalmist's life being burned to ashes. He allowed the world around him to melt his life to the ground, and he desperately needed to be picked up out of the dirt and raised again.

This is my paraphrase of these verses: "I feel burned to the ground. I'm eating dirt. I need life from Your Word. I confess to You my errors, and You teach me again. Give me understanding once again; show me wow things so that I can stop clinging to the dirt around me."

Now, back to what I mentioned earlier about experiencing devastating loss. I wrote this journal entry about twelve or thirteen years before I experienced the most difficult circumstances I've had in my life so far:

While things are going well right now, I hope to file this lesson away. I'm sure that at some point in my life, I will be eating dirt. I don't know what, when, or how, but I know it will happen, and when it does, I want to be prepared.

—From Joe's journal

I had no idea what the most difficult patch in my life would be. I thought I knew what bad things were, but they were only a warm-up. When we lost our daughter Sarah, who was eighteen, in a tragic car accident, then I knew what the psalmist meant about clinging to the dirt. I finally understood what it meant to have your life seemingly burned to the ground. This lesson about what the Word of God can do when I am melted, burned down to the ground, saved me from a life of bitterness, doubt, prolonged depression, and years of wandering in a drunken stupor with personal grief as my excuse.

The psalmist admitted he held too tightly to the things of the world, that he clung to dirt, and it crushed him. This ties into our theme of needing to separate from certain things, which we discussed in the previous chapter.

The author of this psalm was a man who loved God and never missed an opportunity to worship Him. He loved His Word and His people. And yet, he felt as though his life had been burned to the ground.

That's a very different message from the one we get from many preachers today who tell us that if we just trust Jesus, everything will be fine. As long as we do what's right, we'll make money, we'll be happy, and our relationships will thrive.

Wrong! Sometimes our lives are burned to the ground even though we love God's Word and seek to make Heavenly Dad smile. Sometimes your world collapses around you, and it's completely out of your control.

Restored to Green Pastures

To avoid feeling "melted," I desperately need God's Word. I must keep truth flowing fresh and free in my life. It strengthens me, keeps my soul free from loving the dust. When my soul is in the dirt, the only rescue is to let go of it and cling to the "wow things" in the Word of God.

—From Joe's journal

Remove from me the way of lying, and grant me Your law graciously. I have chosen the way of truth; Your judgments I have laid before me. I cling to Your testimonies; O LORD, do not put me to shame! I will run the course of Your commandments, for You shall enlarge my heart.

—Psalm 119:29–32 *(NKJV)*

As we continue with this idea of spiritual discipline and learning to love God's Word, I want to be up-front with you: spending time in God's Word does not mean we will no longer experience hard times or struggles.

Loving God's Word isn't some sort of prosperity message or gospel of easy living. Those are lies, and people end up bitterly disappointed. They get shoved into praise and worship situations where they act like they love God's Word. That can look a lot like a relationship with God to other people.

But that relationship has to work even when things aren't going our way. If you only love God and His Word when you're able to pay your bills and no one you love is sick or dying, you are still, in fact, clinging to the dust and you don't even know it. You're clinging to circumstances rather than truth because you're looking to cling to tangible, temporary things, as we discussed in the previous chapter.

Even if we cling to experiences, possessions, and relationships in the name of Jesus, they will turn to dust. Those things are not His Word. Then we feel betrayed by God when those things turn to dust.

Our hope was in a circumstance or an outcome. We thought, *"If I just do these things, God will give me the outcome I desire."* That's not clinging to the Word. That's clinging to dirt.

Clinging to God's Word will help you keep life's best and worst of things in proper perspective. Instead of clinging to dirt, dust, and temporary things that will always disappoint you, you are able to cling to eternal things, those wow things we learned about last chapter.

It is here we find abundant life—life running in the wide-open, green pasture, even as the temporal world around us is burning to the ground. Because of this, even in the darkest times, we can with integrity tell people that we're thriving.

Let me reveal to you more about my darkest time. After my wife and I lost our daughter in that car accident, three months later, the lead pastor in our church told me he didn't want me around anymore, so I resigned. I was devasted. The two things I clung to the most, my family and my ministry, were ripped form me. Now suddenly we were grieving and unemployed.

If the gospel was about prosperity, none of that would've happened—or when it happened, I would have had plenty of money and having a job wouldn't have mattered. My daughter would still be alive. Trust me, I know what it's like to be in the dust.

While we were grieving and hurting, however, I can honestly say, we were still thriving and running in God's wide-open pasture. That might sound ridiculous, but it was only possible because we were clinging to God's Word, to the wow things in Scripture.

Our circumstances were horrific—there's no minimizing that. We had been completely let down by the world, and even the church. But yet, the following verses explain the miracle that happened in our lives as we navigated these circumstances while clinging to God's Word:

> *Do not be anxious about anything, but in everything by prayer and supplication with thanksgiving let your requests be made known to God. And the peace of God, which surpasses all understanding, will guard your hearts and your minds in Christ Jesus.*
>
> **—Philippians 4:6–7**

The peace of God, which surpasses rational thought and logical conclusions, keeps you in His pasture.

What I'm sharing is not theory; I've experienced it. At that time, I remembered my studies of Psalm 119 twelve years earlier. As I went through that pain, I remembered verse 25: "My soul clings to the dust; revive me according to Your word" (NKJV). And I went back and looked through my journal.

Remember how I wrote, *"While things are going well right now, I hope to file this lesson away. I'm sure that at some point in my life, I will be eating dirt"?* After rereading that, I realized that for my wife, my son, and me to get through this, we had to let go of the dust and cling to wow things, eternal things.

Even in the midst of suffering and hardship, we were running free in God's wide-open pasture. We were thriving while we were hurting. His Word gave us a comfort and peace that sorrow and grief could not take away.

> *Know that the LORD, He is God; it is He who has made us, and not we ourselves; we are His people and the sheep of*

His pasture.

—Psalm 100:3 (NKJV)

Being in God's pasture means abundant living. This is an encouraging verse in difficult situations. When things are hard, it's important that we know what the wow things really are and cling to what is eternal instead of what is temporary. Jesus speaks about this:

I am the door. If anyone enters by me, he will be saved and will go in and out and find pasture. The thief comes only to steal and kill and destroy. I came that they may have life and have it abundantly.
—John 10:9–10

Where is that abundant life? It's in God's pasture.

The world is a thief that seeks to kill you and destroy your soul, to melt it to the ground with grief and sorrow with the deception of temporary comfort and satisfaction. It's so tempting to give into these things that without God's truth permeating your life beforehand, you will grab hold every time. We are tempted to run to and cling to dirt every time because it promises to be satisfying for a while.

Abundant life in God's pasture is different. His pasture can be defined as our connection to His truth, to His wow things that sustain our spiritual lives regardless of our earthly circumstances.

Devotional: Let Go of the Dirt

We have a natural tendency to look for pasture in things we can touch and feel, experience, and control, whether it's circumstances or people. Even if we find rest for a time in these things, clinging to them is clinging to dirt since, as we saw in our Hebrew word study, they will eventually return to dust. That is why our souls often feel as though they are clinging to the dust—because they are! That is what our souls are inclined to do unless they are being permeated by God's Word. His Word is the coolant in the radiator of our souls, a fresh, continuous flow of spiritual truth. As we drive down life's highway of pain, sorrow, and disappointment, the Word of God filters these things, giving us a connection with God that sustains our spirit and helps us to keep our cool, no matter how hot life gets.

In the first four stanzas of Psalm 119, the psalmist asked God to help him fall out of love with the world and in love with God's Word. It culminates with this picture of clinging to dust when the world around us ultimately falls apart. In the next four stanzas, the psalmist moves to a new theme, explaining how he intends to do this by outlining daily checklists for himself. I can honestly say these checklists changed my life.

But for now, "I cling to Your testimonies; O LORD, do not put me to shame! I will run the course of Your commandments, for You shall enlarge my heart" (Psalm 119:31–32 NKJV).

Instead of an expectation that circumstances or events or things will work out, what we need in our relationship with Heavenly Dad is simply an understanding of His Word and a confidence that no matter what life brings us, He will put us into His pasture of abundant life.

It's time to let go of the dirt, cling to God's truth, and find pasture.

WORKBOOK

Chapter Four Questions

Question: Describe a difficult situation you have faced or are facing. Did you draw closer to God through that trial or become more distant from Him? Did His Word comfort and anchor you during your suffering, and if so, how?

_____

_____

_____

_____

_____

_____

_____

_____

_____

_____

Question: What are some things you cling to that have the potential to dissolve into dust and ashes? What is your natural response when something you love is threatened or lost? How can you appreciate these things while still keeping God Himself at the center of your worship and affections?

_____

_____

_____

_____

_____

_____

_____

_____

_____

_____

_____

Question: How do you observe Christianity being promoted as a means for earthly peace and prosperity? Why is this view unbiblical? What does the Bible teach about the various causes of suffering as well as God's relationship to us in the midst of it?

_____

_____

_____

_____

_____

_____

_____

_____

_____

_____

_____

_____

Action: Read a biography or memoir or listen to a podcast about a Christian, past or present, who went through exceptional suffering but was able to thrive throughout that time because of their relationship with God and the hope they found in His Word. What can you learn from their life to help you through your own seasons of hardship?

_____

_____

_____

_____

_____

_____

_____

_____

Chapter Four Notes

CHAPTER FIVE

He—Prayer

I'd like to try to recreate for you a pivotal time in my walk with Jesus. I had worked my way through the first four stanzas of Psalm 119, recording my thoughts in my journal. Then, I came to the stanza titled "He," that changed the way I prayed!

Have you ever experienced God giving you a whole string of incredible, enlightening things as you spend time with Him? For eight days in a row, I was completely, utterly amazed. God was answering the prayer I had learned the week before about opening my eyes to wow things, to the wondrous things in His Word.

This was a time when God's Word revolutionized my view of prayer. The lessons I learned from this passage relieved me of years of religious burden regarding prayer that kept my heart heavy and guilt-ridden.

Teach me, O LORD, the way of Your statutes, and I shall keep it to the end. Give me understanding, and I shall keep Your law; indeed, I shall observe it with my whole heart. Make me walk in the path of Your commandments, for I delight in it. Incline my heart to Your testimonies, and not to covetousness. Turn away my eyes from looking at worthless things, and revive me in Your way. Establish Your word to Your servant, who is devoted to fearing You. Turn away my reproach which I dread, for Your judgments are good. Behold, I long for Your precepts; revive me in Your righteousness.

—Psalm 119:33–40 *(NKJV)*

It dawned on me as I studied this stanza that it was made up of short, one-sentence prayers. I was so impacted by this; I remember crying as I wrote in my journal the day after I finished that section:

For years, prayer has intimidated me. I can't pray for thirty seconds without my mind wandering. I hear about people who pray for an hour a day—I can't do anything for an hour, let alone pray. But today suddenly that burden has been lifted. This passage has taught me what an effective prayer time can look like, and it isn't a marathon. Thank you, God!

—From Joe's journal

There's nothing wrong with long times of prayer, but some of us just aren't wired that way. When I'm reading something, I often find myself having to reread a sentence multiple times because I get distracted. My prayer life was like that, too, and it was a heavy burden.

Here I was a pastor, working in ministry, and I couldn't focus enough to pray for an hour at a time. I remember wondering what was wrong with me—and thinking that when the congregation found out about this, I'd be done for. I suffered in ashamed, ADHD silence.

Rereading my journal reminded me of how my heart was soaring every day as I dove into God's Word. I was only reading one verse a day, but God was showing me wow things. They were so *wow* that I still use them today, and I want you to know them too.

Theological: Six Short Prayers

Through this stanza, God gave me six very short prayers I pray almost every day. It takes me about thirty seconds, and it has revolutionized my life.

Prayer #1

"Teach me, God. It won't be a waste." This is derived from verses 33–34: "Teach me, O LORD, the way of Your statutes, and I shall keep it to the end. Give me understanding, and I shall keep Your law; indeed, I shall observe it with my whole heart" (NKJV).

If we truly desire to learn and increase in our knowledge and application of God's Word, doesn't it make sense to beg God for understanding? This goes back to my prayer for God to open my eyes to wow things. He answered that prayer right here in this passage!

Why wouldn't we ask God for understanding every time we open His Word? The best way to understand it is to ask the Author Himself what He means.

Prayer #2

"God, make me obey Your Word. When I do, my life is so much better." This is taken from verse 35: "Make me walk in the *path* of Your commandments, for I delight in it" (NKJV, emphasis added).

The word translated as "path" is the Hebrew *nathiyb*, which indicates a well-traveled groove.[19] The psalmist prayed that God would make him walk in His path, that He would force him to make a well-traveled groove through His Word. He had such an intense desire to be obedient to what he was learning that he begged God to force him to walk rightly.

How much pain could you have spared yourself in life if you had been praying that prayer from a young age? We must be willing to pray this prayer, to ask God to set up a wall on our left and on our right so that we will not stray from the path of His commandments.

Prayer #3

One of the best Christmas gifts I ever received was a three-dollar backscratcher. My wife gave it to me, and boy, do I love that thing! This gift is so useful and effective: whenever my back itches, it's ingrained in me to grab my backscratcher and scratch my back. By nature, I am now inclined to keep it by my bed, because I know I'll need it at night.

"God, make it natural for me to love Your Word more than temporary stuff." This is from verses 36–37: "*Incline my heart to Your testimonies, and not to covetousness. Turn away my eyes from looking at worthless things, and revive me in Your way*" (NKJV, emphasis added).

The word "incline" here is the Hebrew word *natah*, which carries the idea of being influenced by an outside force of nature[20] in order to make a new direction our natural instinct. This is sort of like how an arborist or a gardener might *incline* a branch to grow a certain direction through pruning or tying it off. The psalmist is asking God to influence him to have a natural inclination to love God's Word.

The psalmist asked God to change his nature—to make it a natural thing for him to enjoy, desire, understand, and love the Word of God. In that same verse, the psalmist recognized and confessed his true nature was covetousness, or looking at and enjoying temporary things. He addressed the continuing struggle, the conflict, between loving God's Word and loving the world.

The psalmist's solution was to ask God to make it natural for him to enjoy God's Word and unnatural for him to be distracted by the things of the world. He wanted a new nature.

It should be abnormal and unnatural for something to become more enjoyable to us than God's Word. It's okay for us to enjoy the things in this world, but we need to keep perspective that eternal things are more important and more desirable. Our prayer is our eyes would be naturally inclined to gaze upon eternal things rather than temporary ones.

Prayer #4

"Confirm the power of Your Word to me, Lord. It excites and motivates me." This is from verse 38: "*Establish* Your word to Your servant, who is devoted to fearing You" (NKJV, emphasis added).

The Hebrew word translated as "establish" is *quwm*.[21] The best way to understand the meaning of this word is confirming something through experimentation

The psalmist asked God to show him, to reassure him of the truth and the reality of the power of God's Word. He desperately needed God to confirm His Word to him through practical experience.

We need to pray this prayer so that we can see the truth of God's Word become reality instead of untested principles. It frustrates me when people preach or otherwise share about pie-in-the-sky concepts and never explain how to apply them. The psalmist wanted God to take the things that he was learning in His Word and confirm them in his everyday life. He wanted to see them and experience them.

When I first read this stanza, I was completely amazed. The week before, I had been praying for God to show me the wow things in His Word. And every day the following week, God gave me these new prayers in this passage. When I saw the Hebrew definition of this word meant "to confirm through a process of testing," it was revolutionary. I had never thought about God's Word that way before. The psalmist is saying, "God, please prove to me again and again that I can trust Your Word"

Though this is an easy prayer to pray, it requires we trust that God's Word is true and allow ourselves to test its precepts. This is one of the many reasons it's so important to make sure you're getting good, biblically solid teaching from your pastors and Bible teachers.

Prayer #5

"Protect me from my own sinful ways. I hate them, but I know Your Word is good." This prayer is derived from verse 39: "Turn away my reproach which I dread, for Your judgments are good" (NKJV).

Reproach is another word for sin. The psalmist hated his sin. He couldn't stand how it was destroying his life and the people in his life. He wanted God to protect him from his sin.

This one really resonated with me, becoming my favorite out of these six prayer sentences. I need protection from myself, my mind and my flesh—my desires, my motives, my inefficiencies, my insufficiencies, and my weaknesses. I need God to protect me from my sinfulness. By praying this prayer every day, I learned to detest my sin and love God's Word.

Prayer #6

"Make me excited and alive concerning Your righteousness." This is taken from verse 40: "Behold, I long for Your precepts; revive me in Your righteousness" (NKJV).

It occurred to me that I need to be just as excited about the power of God's Word in my life, and in the lives of others, as I am about a Buccaneers' touchdown or a slice of meat lover's pizza.

—*From Joe's journal*

This prayer is as powerful as it is simple. Not much needs to be added to explain this. Revive us with Your Word, Lord! Make us alive!

Prayer Leads to Transformation

Imagine what your life would look like if God answered just two of these prayers. What if He answered all of them? What if God started teaching you the truth, made you obey it, made it natural for your heart to hear it and love it more than the things of the world, and confirmed the truth and reality of His Word through your experiences as you tested it?

What if He protected you from your sinful ways, which you learned to hate, and what if the things that excited you and made you alive were righteous things, not worldly things like unhealthy relationships, addictions, money, or possessions? Can you imagine what your life would look like?

These six prayers have evolved a bit over the years, but they are essentially the same as when I started praying them every day over twenty years ago. Each day, I ask God to renew my mind, enlighten me with understanding, make me go in His paths, make it natural for my heart to hear His Word, confirm His Word to me, protect me from my sin, and make me alive in His righteousness. Doing so has changed my life.

Devotional: Take the Prayer Challenge

I want to challenge you to use this daily prayer list. It doesn't have to be a long one, although it may grow over time. You can start by writing these six prayers on an index card and putting it somewhere you'll be sure to see it—on the refrigerator, on your mirror, etc. It'll take you maybe thirty-five to forty-five seconds to go through them all, so you can take your time and focus on each sentence instead of having to rush through them.

I believe that if you pray through this list based on Psalm 119:33–40, there can be no other outcome than immense personal revival. For years, some of you have been hearing sermons about how you need to be different, how you need to change in certain areas. You need to be godlier, you need to be more like Jesus, or you need to do a better job of this or that.

I am offering you a tangible step you can take toward this transformation. This list shows you what to pray for so that you can become more like Christ.

Notice there's nothing on that list about material possessions or worldly success. Also, we aren't interested in prayers for show that look religious, filled with flowery *prayer words*. We desire prayers that create transformation in our hearts. To that end, we will focus on prayers written from, and founded upon, principles in God's Word.

You don't have to wonder how to take the next step. It's right here, waiting for you to take it.

WORKBOOK

Chapter Five Questions

Question: How would you describe your prayer life? Do you find it easy or difficult to concentrate in prayer or to pray for long periods of time? When does prayer come most naturally for you, and when do you most struggle to pray?

_____

_____

_____

_____

_____

_____

_____

_____

_____

_____

_____

Question: Think over the things about which you spend the most time praying. Are they material things/specific blessings, such as financial help, healing, and relief from problems? How often do you pray for spiritual things such as greater obedience, understanding, wisdom, and love for God and His Word?

_____

_____

_____

_____

_____

_____

_____

_____

_____

_____

_____

Question: What are some areas where you need to practically apply the truths of God's Word to everyday situations? What are some ways that you need God to protect you from your own sinful inclinations?

_____

_____

_____

_____

_____

_____

_____

_____

_____

_____

_____

_____

Action: Write out each of the six prayers in your own words, looking at the original meaning in the Hebrew and the author's interpretation of the verse. Begin to pray these six short prayers each day, taking time to think about what each one means and to ask God with humility and sincerity to make this true in your life.

_____

_____

_____

_____

_____

_____

_____

_____

_____

_____

Chapter Five Notes

CHAPTER SIX

Waw—Life in a Wide Place

Often, Christian living seems to be characterized by shame, guilt, paralysis, and a lack of confidence. It's an epidemic. God's Word and the gospel are not designed to leave us sulking, guilt-ridden, and hopelessly overwhelmed with religious burdens. To escape this paralysis, we need to understand our connection with God should leave us confident, free, and living in a wide place. This wide place comes as a result of the things we've been learning, as we will see in this sixth stanza, titled "Waw:"

*Let Your mercies come also to me, O LORD—Your salvation according to Your word. So shall I have an answer for him who reproaches me, for I trust in Your word. And take not the word of truth utterly out of my mouth, for I have hoped in Your ordinances. So shall I keep Your law continually, forever and ever. And I will walk **at liberty**, for I seek Your precepts. I will speak of Your testimonies also before kings, and will not be **ashamed**. And I will delight myself in Your commandments, which I love. My hands also I will lift up to Your commandments, which I love, and I will meditate on Your statutes.*
—Psalm 119:41–48 *(NKJV)*

Confidence is being able to stay with God's Word no matter what my circumstances. It is not the fleshly reaction to conflict that I'm so used to, trying to intimidate or outshout someone, trying to out-stubborn them, which I'm really good at. Confidence is when my actions and my attitudes say that I believe the Word of God to be true.

—From Joe's journal

In this chapter, we'll be talking about confidence. I'm giving it a synonym: *the wide place.*

Historical: Hebrew Word Study

The word translated as "at liberty" in verse 45, what the ESV calls the "wide place," is the Hebrew *rachab*, which describes a wide place that is roomy in every direction.[22] Being in the wide place means being wide in liberty and confidence.

"Ashamed" in verse 46 is the Hebrew word *buwsh*, which means to be disappointed or shamed, to be confounded or restrained by fear.[23] Notice the contrast between a place of shame or restraint and a place of wide living.

Clearly the psalmist is making a comparison. Because of God's Word, he declares he has the freedom to do what is right, to live freely, and to speak before kings. Compare this to a life shackled by guilt, shame, confusion, and religious burdens.

What does life in a wide place look like? How do you know if you're living there? I will describe this life—which is still a life with mistakes and failures—in contrast to a life of shame, disappointment, and shackles.

What do you think the gospel, and a connection with Heavenly Dad, is designed to provide in the first place? Religious guilt? Fear? A relationship that feels like there's always someone looking over your shoulder, just waiting to zap you?

Theological: Three Kinds of Confidence

Life in a wide place provides several different areas of confidence. The psalmist declares these different areas of confidence and points to his relationship with the Word of God as the reason for it.

1. The first area of confidence is confidence in connection (vv. 41–43). This is the confidence to break from the traditions of religion or society because you are connected to Heavenly Dad.

Here's a great example of this from the life of the psalmist, who I believe is David. To provide some context, David was on the run from Saul, who was trying to kill him because Saul was afraid David would take his throne. David and a few of his men traveled to Nob to visit Ahimelek the priest, and they were desperately in need of provisions.

"Now therefore, what have you on hand? Give me five loaves of bread in my hand, or whatever can be found."

And the priest answered David and said, 'There is no common bread on hand; but there is holy bread, if the young men have at least kept themselves from women."

Then David answered the priest, and said to him, 'Truly, women have been kept from us about three days since I came out. And the vessels of the young men are holy, and the bread is in effect common, even though it was consecrated in the vessel this day."

So the priest gave him holy bread; for there was no bread there but the showbread which had been taken from before the LORD, in order to put hot bread in its place on the

day when it was taken away.
—*1 Samuel 21:3–6 (NKJV)*

The holy bread would have previously been in the tabernacle in the presence of the Lord (Exodus 25:30). Once it was replaced with fresh bread, it was taken out of the tabernacle and given to the priests to eat (Leviticus 24:5–9). Only the priests were allowed to eat this bread.

David, however, wasn't intimidated by religion. He had a connection with God. He knew God's Word, and he was confident about the purpose of the law, which is to bring people to God, not to condemn them and treat them as though they will never be able to connect with Him. The law is meant to help us recognize our need for grace and mercy.

David knew his connection to Heavenly Dad didn't depend on how good a Jew he was but on the gift of faith. While others may have been aghast at what he was about to do, his confidence enabled him to live in a wide place. David was struggling and in a desperate situation, but he had confidence to take what he needed and to live free from legalism and religious rules that could have caused him to miss out on God's blessings and provision.

There is therefore now no condemnation for those who are in Christ Jesus.
—*Romans 8:1*

This confidence in our connection to Heavenly Dad means no matter what happens in life, we can know our connection with Him is not based on our religious ability to hold onto Him but on His ability to hold onto us. You must have confidence in your connection.

2. *The second area of confidence that comes from*

living in a wide place is confidence when you are tempted.
This is the confidence to do right regardless of your circumstances because of your relationship with the Word of God. You have confidence God will honor your righteousness as well as confidence He already knows about and sees your unrighteousness.

We may fail in the area of temptation, but this is where the connection with Heavenly Dad and living in a wide place becomes supernatural. When we do fail, we retreat to humility, not guilt. Guilt is a sign of living in a narrow, restricted place; this is the place of shame the psalmist makes refence to in the last third of this stanza. Humility is the result of living in a wide, liberated, free place.

If your humility doesn't produce joy and fresh starts, it's not humility. It's merely guilt without forgiveness, which always results in shame. You aren't living in a wide place if you are burdened with guilt and shame.

One of the biggest mistakes Christians make is focusing on our depravity over the greatness of God and His mercy, which causes us to step out of the wide place. Perpetual religious sulking and guilt are at odds with true humility, brokenness, and liberty.

The former focuses on your failures instead of Christ's victory. It leads to religion that lacks confidence, a life of endless cycles of emotional highs and valleys of guilt as we cycle through times of failure and despair.

While guilt leads to condemnation and defeat, biblical humility—which is a result of the gift of faith—produces dependence and trust. Humility says, "I can't do this on my own. I need Heavenly Dad." Guilt says, "I'm so bad that no one can ever love me."

In many respects, guilt is selfish and shackling. It's a narrow place. Humility leads to freedom. It is a wide place.

Hebrews 4:16 reminds us, "Let us then with confidence draw near to the throne of grace, that we may receive mercy and find grace to help in time of need."

In your time of need, in your time of failure, have confidence to draw near to grace—not paralysis that says, "Woe is me," but confidence that says, "Wow, that proves it again. I can't do it on my own. Here I come, Dad."

When we do fail, we can continue because of confidence we have in our connection in God. That is what gives us confidence when we are tempted.

3. The third area of confidence that comes from living in a wide place is confidence in wisdom. Understanding the world from a biblical perspective gives us innately wise counsel and enables us to speak truth to anyone at any time and in any circumstances, just as the psalmist was able to speak to kings. The purpose of wisdom, however, is not to win arguments but to teach us how to bless others.

According to James 1:5, "If any of you lacks wisdom, let him ask God, who gives generously to all without reproach, and it will be given him." Those who humbly submit to God and lean on Him for wisdom will receive true insight because they rely on the very Author of reality. True wisdom is found in the Bible, God's Word, and those who depend on it will not be steered wrong. However, those who do not follow God's Word are always struggling to patch together a coherent worldview. James 1:6 likens a person who doubts to "a wave of the sea that is driven and tossed by the wind." They are not anchored in anything and therefore lack confidence, so they are tossed about by each storm they face and have nothing wise to say.

When the truth needs to be proclaimed, you are not intimidated into silence because you have confidence in the Author of truth and its veracity has been confirmed to you by God, which is one prayer we talked about in the previous chapter. It has been confirmed to you, and you understand God's opinion on the matter must be dealt with.

Wisdom in the wide place is not arrogant, combative, judgmental, or political. It's a humble, supernatural confidence that gives you credibility, a direct result of the gift of faith that has been nurtured through a connection with God's Word, because you understand His law, His counsel, His precepts, His judgments, and His rhythm of righteousness.

It's wisdom with the goal of shepherding with truth, not the goal of winning.

> *Therefore, we are ambassadors for Christ, God making his appeal through us. We implore you on behalf of Christ, be reconciled to God. For our sake he made him to be sin who knew no sin, so that in him we might become the righteousness of God.*
>
> **—2 Corinthians 5:20-21**

Ambassadors are often sent to speak to people who are in positions of power, which lines up with what the psalmist said about having confidence to speak to kings (v. 46).

Those are the three areas of confidence we develop by living in a wide place: confidence in connection, confidence in temptation, and confidence in wisdom.

Life in a Wide Place Versus Life in the Place of Shame

David lived in a wide place. He expressed this concept repeatedly throughout the psalms he wrote:

> *He also brought me out into a broad place; He delivered me because He delighted in me.*
>
> **—Psalm 18:19** *(NKJV)*

And [You] have not shut me up into the hand of the enemy;
You have set my feet in a wide place.

—Psalm 31:8 *(NKJV)*

This is one reason I think David wrote Psalm 119. He loved using this image of a wide, broad place. This was a man who lied and committed adultery, murder, and countless other sins. If anyone deserved to live in a narrow, confined, shackled place, it was him.

David certainly experienced the consequences of his sins. His life was filled with incredible hardship, including his son Absalom despising him and trying to usurp his throne. The wide place is not a prosperity gospel that guarantees an easy life. There were issues in David's life that were harmful and painful, yet he still lived his life in a wide place.

Can you see the difference between life lived in a wide place and life lived in shame, between guilt and humility? I could've included many other journal entries in this chapter in which I confessed my flaws and my sin to Heavenly Dad in humility. They will not be seen until after I die, but I guarantee that if you were to read them, you would wonder how I could possibly have any confidence to stand before my congregation and preach Sunday after Sunday.

I'll tell you how: because I live in a wide place. The time I have spent in God's Word has allowed me to live there. God has made it clear that He has not called me to depression, religious sulking, guilt, or discouragement. He has called me to live with the reality of the issues and flaws in my life. I can acknowledge them because I know God already knows about them.

But while I live with the reality of these flaws and issues, God, through His Word, has enabled me to understand and trust His cure for them. His cure puts me in a wide place. He reminds me I'm connected to Him; He protects me from my own reproach (v. 39), and He gives me wisdom to teach truth.

As a pastor, I so badly want to see people set free in a wide place—to have confidence in their connection with God, in their righteousness through Christ, and in wisdom they have gained from His Word. You can find that wide place in a life in which God's Word permeates your heart and your mind.

Devotional: Living in Grace

It's time for us to live in a wide place. That's what "the GraceLife" I wrote about in my first book is all about: it's a synonym for living in a wide place. It's not about perfection. No one is perfect, and we all live with the reality of our flaws, mistakes we have made, and the hurt we have caused others.

Though we acknowledge those things, we don't live in guilt, because guilt indicates we don't understand grace. Humility and brokenness produce connection to God, which in turn produces confidence in temptation and confidence to speak truth.

I don't want to guilt anyone into spending time with God's Word. I want you to be motivated into spending time with His Word, to begin to desire life in a wide place. How do you do that? By praying through the prayer list in the previous chapter and reading the Word of God more.

When I began my study of Psalm 119, I was tired of just coasting through Christianity. I was ready to live in a wide place. I pray the same for you.

It's time to put off shame, religious sulking, and guilt. Live in a wide place with confidence, because we know the reality of our sin, but we trust God's cure for it.

Chapter Six Questions

Question: Are there areas where you feel bound by legalism? What are some verses that specifically speak to the confidence a believer can have in their relationship with their Heavenly Dad? How can this relationship set you free from a life of rules and bondage?

_____

_____

_____

_____

_____

_____

_____

_____

_____

_____

Question: Which word best describes your approach to God, guilt, or humility? Are you more focused on your failures or Christ's victory? How will you allow failure to prompt you to humbly seek God's help instead of wallowing in guilt and regret?

_____

_____

_____

_____

_____

_____

_____

_____

_____

_____

Question: Read James 1:5–8. Describe a time when you were able to speak confidently in sharing wisdom from God's Word. Describe a time you kept silent because you did not know or understand the Scriptures. Does your attitude—in person and on social media if applicable— suggest that you are more interested in winning arguments and being right or in gently shepherding others toward truth?

_____

_____

_____

_____

_____

_____

_____

_____

_____

_____

_____

Action: Write down the barriers that are keeping you from living in a wide place. Do you carry guilt or shame over past sins? Crippling lists of do's and don'ts? Beside each barrier, write down a Scripture passage that knocks out that barrier and sets you free to live in the wide place of confidence that God has for you.

_____

_____

_____

_____

_____

_____

_____

_____

Chapter Six Notes

_____

_____

_____

_____

_____

_____

_____

_____

_____

_____

_____

_____

_____

_____

_____

_____

_____

_____

_____

_____

_____

CHAPTER SEVEN

Zayin—Tassels for Remembering

In our process of learning to love God's Word, it's important we remember things. That's the focus of the seventh stanza of Psalm 119, titled "Zayin."

Remember the word to Your servant, upon which You have caused me to hope. This is my comfort in my affliction, for Your word has given me life. The proud have me in great derision, yet I do not turn aside from Your law. I remembered Your judgments of old, O LORD, and have comforted myself.

Indignation has taken hold of me because of the wicked, who forsake Your law. Your statutes have been my songs In the house of my pilgrimage. I remember Your name in the night, O LORD, and I keep Your law. This has become mine, because I kept Your precepts.
—Psalm 119:49–56 *(NKJV)*

Our memory is often a slave to the past, causing a lot of problems for us.

I have painful memories from just two years ago, filled with feelings of anger, revenge, failure, and many other things. I remember being stripped of my self-worth and confidence. I remember feeling sick to my stomach. I remember sitting in church, sobbing uncontrollably. I remember crying out to God, begging Him to take the pain away—and Father, You certainly did that.

It all started when I began to remember God's Word. I remember times of prayer. I remember God providing me a teaching job. I remember God giving me the dream of coaching a football team and going undefeated. I remember God bringing people into my life who loved me and restored my confidence. I remember God leading me to this church I'm in right now and giving me this job as a pastor. I remember God giving me a wife in that church. I remember those works of old. I remember all the things I have learned, the 'wow things' in Your Word since that time.

I remember all the times I needed cleansing, and You granted it. I remember praising You once I realized all You had done for me. I remember. I am moved to tears now just thinking about how You are healing and blessing me, how You lifted me out of darkness and put me in a wide place. I will always remember all these works of old and be strengthened by these memories, how You confirmed Your Word to me. It will renew my strength to get through the pain that will inevitably come in the future. No matter what it is, I will face it with confidence, remembering my gracious God and His precious Word. That is my source of strength.

—From Joe's journal

This idea of remembering is threaded throughout Scripture: remembering God's Word, remembering truth, and remembering what God has done in your life.

Something tells me that might be a very important concept—one that God wants us to remember! Unfortunately, this generally requires a bit of discipline and effort.

Historical: The Impact of Remembering God's Word

Why should we bother remembering God's Word? There are two crucial benefits of remembering God's Word:

1. It serves as a warning system. Here's an example from the life of David, as described in 1 Samuel 24.

God had chosen David to replace Saul as king. Saul was so angry and jealous, he wanted to kill David before he replaced Saul and became king. David fled Jerusalem, and Saul pursued him into the wilderness with an army of three thousand men to find and kill him to keep him from taking the throne. They couldn't find David anywhere because he went into hiding with his mighty men.

Saul had to relieve himself, so he went into a cave—the same cave David and his men happened to be hiding in! David's men encouraged him to take advantage of this vulnerable moment and kill Saul, saying the Lord was delivering Saul into David's hand.

David grabbed his knife and crept up behind Saul. He could kill him, and all his worries would be over. Then he saw the corner of Saul's robe. Jewish men wore tassels on the corners of their robe to remind them of God's Word.

Again the LORD spoke to Moses, saying, "Speak to the children of Israel: Tell them to make tassels on the corners of their garments throughout their generations, and to put a blue thread in the tassels of the corners. And you shall have the tassel, that you may look upon it and remember all the commandments of the LORD and do them, and that you may not follow the harlotry to which your own heart and

*your own eyes are inclined, and that you may remember
and do all My commandments, and be holy for your God."*
—Numbers 15:37–40 *(NKJV)*

David secretly cut off the corner of Saul's robe, and as
Saul was leaving the cave, David followed and called out
to him. He held up the corner of the robe, "I could have
killed you, but far be it from me to touch the LORD's
anointed." Saul might have been wearing the tassels designed to remind him of God's precepts, but he forgot to
conduct himself according to God's Word. David, however, remembered.

*Incline my heart to Your testimonies, and not to covetous-
ness. Turn away my eyes from looking at worthless things,
and revive me in Your way.*
—Psalm 119:36–37 *(NKJV)*

There's a two-sided picture here: David remembered
God's Word, and Saul forgot it. I believe as David looked
at those tassels, he remembered, and he realized he would
have been disqualified from being king if he had killed
Saul.

This a wonderful historical example of how remembering God's Word functions as a warning system. It can
warn us about what not to do and what to avoid.

2. God's Word provides a springboard to praise: "I remember the days of old; I meditate on all Your works; I
muse on the work of Your hands. I spread out my hands
to You; my soul longs for You like a thirsty land" (Psalm
143:5–6 NKJV).

That's exactly what was happening in my journal entry—remembering what God had done for me and
meditating on His works.

*And remember that you were a slave in the land of Egypt,
and the LORD your God brought you out from there by a
mighty hand and by an outstretched arm; therefore the
LORD your God commanded you to keep the Sabbath day.*
—Deuteronomy 5:15 *(NKJV)*

*Remember His marvelous works which He has done, His
wonders, and the judgments of His mouth, O seed of Israel
His servant, You children of Jacob, His chosen ones!*
—1 Chronicles 16:12–13 *(NKJV)*

When we remember God's Word and His works, it
gives us objective evidence to praise Him—not just during a worship service but in all areas of life. The whole
core, the key, and the foundation of knowing how to
praise God is remembering who He is, what He has done,
and what He has said in His Word.

Theological: Reprogramming Our Memories

Here's the problem: our memories likely need to be reprogrammed. My memory is filled with junk and garbage.
Memories that harm me instead of benefiting me, memories that hold me hostage almost daily. Memories ravaged
by my sin, pain, and betrayal. Memories riddled with disappointment and personal failure. It embarrasses me, and
I'm shackled to it.

These memories cause me to obsess over my failures,
blinding me to what God is doing in my life. Sometimes
all we can think about are the negative things in our memories, and we miss what He's doing right here, right now.

So we search for good memories, fixating on temporal
fantasy trinkets. Paging through our high school yearbooks, social media timelines, reminiscing on how good
things were back then. We keep temporal tokens of a

vacation with friends because of how much fun we had then.

We start to put our hope and trust in these temporal trinkets, but they are powerless to transform our minds. We become slaves to the past with only an occasional temporary relief of endorphins. This approach will never reprogram our memories: "Do not say, 'Why were the former days better than these?' For you do not inquire wisely concerning this" (Ecclesiastes 7:10 NKJV).

To turn your memory into a powerful tool, transform it and reprogram it by filling it with the Word of God and the works of His hands: "I remembered Your judgments of old, O LORD, and have comforted myself" (Psalm 119:52 NKJV).

As we learned in Chapter One, this starts with diligent inquiry into Scripture. We must create a memory of what we learn, the wow things that God gives us. They will serve to help us focus on God and His glory during the night—*the night* meaning difficult times: "I remember Your name in the night, O LORD, and I keep Your law" (Psalm 119:55 NKJV).

This means when the night hits, the first thing you do is remember Heavenly Dad's truth and run to His arms, taking comfort in what He has said, what He has done, and what He has promised to do. That's what my family and I did when we experienced the tragic loss of our daughter in 2007.

You begin to have the ability to recall instructions from God's Word: "This has become mine, because I kept Your precepts" (Psalm 119:56 NKJV).

As the Word of God reprograms your memory, you will naturally focus on Him during the difficult times. When I think about the difficulties I've experienced over the last twenty years, what I remember most is what God did in me, for me, and through me during those times, far more than the pain I experienced!

In addition, having a memory of the wow things God has given you from Scripture replaces those toxic memories of guilt, shame, and embarrassment with grace, mercy, and comfort: "Do not be conformed to this world, but be transformed by the renewal of your mind, that by testing you may discern what is the will of God, what is good and acceptable and perfect" (Romans 12:2). In 2 Corinthians 5:17, Paul reminds us: "If anyone is in Christ, he is a new creation. The old has passed away; behold, the new has come." God's Word enables us to trust this and remember it in a way that supersedes the memory of our failures.

Devotional: Finding Your Tassels

In my life, I need tassels to remind me of the commandments of God. I need something to keep the Word of God close to my heart, to keep me mindful to obey the Word of God consistently. I need God to hang tassels on my heart. The only difference between me and the world is how tight a grip the Word of God has on my tablet of flesh.

—From Joe's journal

Remember back to earlier in the chapter when I discussed the tassels that Hebrew men wore to be reminded of God's Word? I encourage you to start making memories of the wow things God is teaching you, whether it's through a sermon series, a book, your time in the Word, or a discussion with friends. If you found a huge diamond, would you just stick it in your closet and forget about it? As Christians, we do this all the time with God's Word. He shows us something amazing, and we just toss it in the proverbial closet and forget about it.

If it were a diamond, you'd put a lot of effort and discipline into preserving it. You would know exactly where it was always, so you could access it when you need it. Unfortunately, we don't really do that when it comes to wow things in Scripture.

Remembering the Word of God and its concepts distinguishes those whom God has called from those who aren't connected to the Father. His Word and its concepts should become part of your thought process.

This is a pivotal part of your journey in learning how to love God's Word. In reality, remembering is the catalyst of this entire book, as I share passages from the journal I kept on my journey. I promise you that if you find the tassels that work for you, these new memories will transform your daily thought process. The way you interact with the world around you will change. You won't be perfect, but you will have an unmistakable new direction.

Remember His marvelous works which He has done, His wonders, and the judgments of His mouth.
—1 Chronicles 16:12 *(NKJV)*

Are you actively doing anything that is helping you do that? This passage from Paul is the secret.

You yourselves are our letter of recommendation, written on our hearts, to be known and read by all. And you show that you are a letter from Christ delivered by us, written not with ink but with the Spirit of the living God, not on tablets of stone but on tablets of human hearts.
—2 Corinthians 3:2–3

We need tassels not on our garments but on our hearts! If you really want to experience the transformational power of God's Word in your life, you must start remembering. For me, what helped was meticulous journaling. You don't have to journal like I did—there are so many ways to remember.

You could jot down wow things on a notepad, type them out on a computer, or write them on notecards and tape them to your bathroom mirror or kitchen cabinets. You could make a sketch, or put them into a song. Your tassels can take whatever form you need them to take. You just need to have them. Otherwise, you will fail to remember, and you will never grow in your faith.

We need a wealth of memories we can draw upon for that early warning system, for the motivation to praise God, and to help survive when times get dark. Without them, you're just like everyone else—a slave to bad memories, antithetical to redemption and transformation.

WORKBOOK

Chapter Seven Questions

Question: Does remembering the past fill you will gratitude and praise or with hurt and regret? How can you change your perspective on those painful memories to trace God's hand and goodness even through those parts of your life you would rather forget?

_____

_____

_____

_____

_____

_____

_____

_____

_____

Question: How can you intentionally remember the insights and teachings of God's Word? How are you committing Scripture to memory? How are you remembering and reviewing the things God shows you from His Word, so they become part of your life, not just lost moments of revelation?

_____

_____

_____

_____

_____

_____

_____

_____

_____

_____

Question: Take time to write out or to share with a friend important milestone memories of God's work in your life. As you contemplate what He has done, note the attributes each reflects, such as His goodness, His mercy, His faithfulness. Use your list as a springboard for thanksgiving and praise.

_____

_____

_____

_____

_____

_____

_____

_____

_____

_____

Action: What are your tassels? How will you actively re-member the wow moments from God's Word and the ways that He works in your life? If you are feeling stumped, try asking a mature Christian friend for ideas. Then begin this week to implement these ideas for inten-tional remembrance into your daily life.

_____

_____

_____

_____

_____

_____

_____

_____

Chapter Seven Notes

CHAPTER EIGHT

Heth—Your Piece of the Pie

To this day, I struggle with pie.[24] As a kid, I always wanted the biggest piece I could possibly get. If I was asked to choose between two  pieces—one which would go to me and the other to my sister—I would choose the larger portion without hesitation. My value system was all about getting what I wanted first. But I didn't understand the Lord is truly my portion and gives me much more than a fleshly reward.

*You are my **portion**, O LORD; I have said that I would keep Your words. I entreated Your favor with my whole heart; be merciful to me according to Your word. I thought about my ways, and turned my feet to Your testimonies. I made haste, and did not delay to keep Your commandments. The cords of the wicked have bound me, but I have not forgotten Your law. At midnight I will rise to give thanks to You, because of Your righteous judgments. I am a companion of all who fear You, and of those who keep Your precepts. The*

earth, O LORD, is full of Your mercy; teach me Your statutes.
—Psalm 119:57–64 *(NKJV, emphasis added)*

This eighth stanza, titled "Heth," is a beautiful description of what life looks like when God is your portion, when He is your pursuit rather than the things of the world. Are you starting to love God's Word as we work our way through Psalm 119? By the end of this chapter, I'm hoping you'll be able to tell one way or the other if this is having an impact on you—kind of like a midterm.

I must determine when my desires are rooted in pursuing selfishness as my portion and when they are pursuing God as my portion, my piece of the pie. While I can enjoy things, my motivation should not be to acquire those things over a deeper relationship with God. This will be evidence by my actions, my schedule, my spending, my relationships, and how I respond to correction and hardship.

—From Joe's journal

Historical: Hebrew Word Study

The Hebrew word translated as "portion" in verse 57 is *cheleq*, which refers to a rightful share or to a tract of land or possession.[25] In Psalm 119, in the context of the other stanzas, it is symbolic of what we value.

This entire psalm is about the value of God's Word, so this verse refers to the fact that the Word of God was what the psalmist desired. It was his portion. Our portion is our piece of the pie. It represents what we desire, what we identify with. It's what we wake up for, what we spend our time and money on.

So, in this context, the word *portion* means passions,

motivations, desires. The Word of God was the psalmist's passion, motivation, desire, and identity. It was what he valued, what he had chosen. David's portion, his piece of the pie, was God's Word. The Lord was his portion. This was the irrevocable choice of his life, and it created undeniable patterns of commitment, communion, correction, and consistency. That same portion will create the same patterns in your life.

Theological: God's Word Will Change Your Values

Once God's Word takes up residence in your heart, your perception of the pie, your piece of it, will begin to change. As you crave and pursue a connection with Him, He will change your values in these six ways.

1. You will find the eternal becomes more important than the temporal. You will begin cherishing the things of heaven more than the things of earth: "You are my portion, O LORD; I have said that I would keep Your words" (Psalm 119:57 NKJV).

We must arrive at the place where it really doesn't matter how big our worldly piece of the pie is. Our hearts and eyes should always be set on our portion, our piece, being with God. This doesn't mean that temporal things aren't part of your life. It just means they are not your portion, your pursuit, your driving passion.

2. The inward becomes more important than the outward. You'll focus on how God sees you rather than how other people see you: "I entreated Your favor with my whole heart; be merciful to me according to Your word. I thought about my ways, and turned my feet to Your testimonies" (Psalm 119:58–59 NKJV).

A true lover of God's Word constantly analyzes and evaluates their life. Introspection is spurred on by the Holy Spirit through the Word of God. Many Christians stop there, ending in paralysis, overwhelming guilt, or depression. That, however, is a sign you don't really love and trust God's Word, because trust in God's Word gives you motivation and confidence to make adjustments when it becomes evident they are needed, the antithesis of paralysis through guilt or shame.

If you read the Word of God and find you need to adjust your life but don't follow through because you are discouraged by how hard it might be, that indicates you love the things needing adjusting more than the standard you're judging them by. A child of God who loves God's Word sees through introspection, through looking inward, what needs to change, then makes the necessary corrections.

3. You will have an immediate response to the need for correction. You will take urgent action when your life doesn't line up with God's Word: "I made haste, and did not delay to keep Your commandments" (Psalm 119:60 NKJV).

It is important for Christians to be connected not only to God's Word but also to His people because He often teaches us His Word through His people. When Christians who are not connected to either God's Word or His people are confronted with sin, they often do not repent or do anything to correct themselves.

David needed both. He knew the Word, but sometimes he needed Nathan, the prophet, to confront him with his sin (2 Samuel 12). If God is our portion, the piece of the pie we crave, we have a sense of urgency to make those corrections in our lives. Whenever David was confronted with his sin—which was often—he responded immediately and willingly received correction.

It's not about perfection. It's about being willing to look inward instead of outward when God's Word reveals you are out of line. You see what God sees, and you're willing to make the necessary corrections, and make them right away.

4. You will no longer fear the dark. Hardships will no longer be excuses. We often use hardships as an excuse for compromising our words or actions, or as an excuse for failure. Having a bad day at work becomes an excuse for yelling at our family. Failing to achieve a goal we set for ourselves becomes an excuse to escape reality through addiction or isolation.

Instead, these should be times when we grow closer and cling harder: "The cords of the wicked have bound me, but I have not forgotten Your law. At midnight I will rise to give thanks to You, because of Your righteous judgments" (Psalm 119:61–62 NKJV).

The psalmist is not talking about a time of day in those verses; he is talking about the times of stress and hardship in our lives. All too often, we tend to interpret those verses as follows: "The cords of the wicked ensnare me, therefore it's okay to slip up. Life's tough! I deserve a twenty-four-hour break from God's Word. Today, my portion of the pie is something different from God at this moment, because life is too hard."

When we are disconnected from God's people and God's Word, we will use stress as an excuse to grab a piece of the selfish pie. A strong connection to God's Word creates obedience and rejoicing, even during the midnight of our lives.

5. You will have healthier relationships. When believers are connected to God's Word and His people, their relationships become less dysfunctional, less codependent, and less destructive: "I am a companion of all who fear You, and of those who keep Your precepts" (Psalm 119:63 NKJV).

Healthy relationships based upon mutual love for the Word of God are stable, enduring, and mutually beneficial. At times, we will fall away from loving God's Word—it will happen—and that's when our relationships become strained and at risk of dysfunction.

These are the self-seeking pie moments that occur when feelings and emotions are most hurt, when connections are strained or severed. That's why obedience without delay, as described in verse 60, is so crucial; otherwise, we leave the door open for the destruction of our healthy, godly relationships.

When that happens, we replace those relationships with new and dangerous ones, with worldly portions of pie. We look for people who have not chosen God as their portion. We will always have relationships. The question is whether they will be based upon a mutual love for God's Word or a mutual affection for the world's pie. When we become disconnected to God's Word or His people, we leave the door open for those relationships to be severed and broken, and we will replace them with destructive ones.

We need these God centered relationships because they help us see our blind spots. We need other people we trust to point these things out. I have people who do this in my life, and they drive me nuts! But I need them, and so do you.

6. *Your values will change because you will choose mercy over entitlement.* This is crucial because it shows God's Word is transforming your heart and values. You will overcome the cancer of bitterness and victimhood: "The earth, O LORD, is full of Your mercy; teach me Your statutes" (Psalm 119:64 NKJV).

When you are learning and remembering the Word of God, you become aware of the ocean of mercy surrounding you. Though we are ever mindful of our sin and its power, it's no longer our obsession. Since we are under God's mercy, our main focus cannot be how unfair the world is, how it cheats us out of our piece of the pie, or how it makes us victims. We also cannot allow the world to influence what type of pie we believe we are entitled to—political, financial, emotional, or material.

Feelings of entitlement and victimhood allow you to justify almost any type of pie you want in your life and to get that pie however you see fit. You can justify deception, selfishness, and even stealing because of that sense of entitlement. After all, you're only doing what you need to do get what's rightfully yours.

It's hard to feel like a victim when you understand mercy. Mercy is our lifeblood, and we don't deserve a drop of it. The piece of the pie we really deserve is judgment, separation, and death, but mercy gives us life, connection, and forgiveness. We don't deserve any of it. We haven't earned it through our religion, our liturgy, our schedule-keeping, or our giving. It has been given to us because of Christ's work on the cross.

This understanding of mercy creates the desire to extend mercy to others, even those who may have wronged us or stolen our former portion to which we thought we were entitled. We're able to say, "You can have that pie. This one tastes better."

Without God's Word constantly flowing into our lives, we live blind to His ocean of mercy. The more time you spend in His Word, the more aware you are of the ocean of mercy surrounding you.

Devotional: What's Your Piece of the Pie?

How you invest your time and money reveals what's important to you. What you watch on TV, what you listen to on the radio or podcasts, what you talk about, what you're willing to spend your hard-earned money on—it all reveals what you consider your piece of the pie.

We're willing to get up at 6 a.m. Monday through Friday to go to work and further our career or go to the gym and further our physical fitness. However, waking up at 9 a.m. on a Sunday to go to church and further our connection with God and His people—well, that's just too early!

If your life feels like a parched desert and you don't let the living waters of God's Word fill it, you will be bare and empty. But when the Word of God is flowing into your life, these six qualities will bloom as God's Word does its work in you.

We need to arrive at a place we salivate emotionally and intellectually for God's Word. You can tell that's happening when the six qualities described in this stanza start to become visible. It won't happen all at once and there will likely be ups and downs. But over time, if you choose mercy over entitlement, you'll notice, for example, that you aren't bitter, or you've become more focused on the eternal than the temporal.

Like the psalmist, you begin to realize all other pies leave you perpetually unsatisfied. You always want more and can never get enough. But now, the Lord is your portion, your piece of the pie, and He never leaves you hungry.

WORKBOOK

Chapter Eight Questions

Question: What is your portion? What do you long for or identify as essential to your sense of self and well-being? Put another way, what in your life would you say you can't live without?

_____

_____

_____

_____

_____

_____

_____

_____

_____

_____

Question: When eternal things are more important than temporal things, how will this be reflected in the daily interactions of a believer's life? Give practical examples of attitudes, decisions, and desires that will change with an eternal perspective.

_____

_____

_____

_____

_____

_____

_____

_____

_____

_____

Question: Does stress lead you to selfishness or to godliness? How can you turn hardship and stress into a trigger for getting closer to God and going deeper into His Word?

_____

_____

_____

_____

_____

_____

_____

_____

_____

_____

Action: It is important for Christians to be connected not only to God's Word but also to His people, because He often teaches us His Word through His people. Who speaks the truth of the Bible into your life? Who could you become better connected with so that this person could teach you more about the Word? Are you open to this wise believer pointing out blind spots in your life? Plan a time to meet with such a mentor figure this week. Share with them what you have been learning from Psalm 119 and ask for their insights into the Scripture as well.

_____

_____

_____

_____

_____

_____

_____

_____

_____

Chapter Eight Notes

CHAPTER NINE

Teth—Affliction Seminar

*You have dealt **well** with Your servant, O LORD, according
to Your word. Teach me good judgment and knowledge,
for I believe Your commandments. Before I was **afflicted** I
went astray, but now I keep Your word. You are good, and
do good; teach me Your statutes. The proud have forged a
lie against me, but I will keep Your precepts with my whole
heart. Their heart is as fat as grease, but I delight in Your
law. It is good for me that I have been **afflicted**, that I may
learn Your statutes. The law of Your mouth is better to me
than thousands of coins of gold and silver.*
—Psalm 119:65–72 *(NKJV, emphasis added)*

The world is tough. It's fallen and riddled with depravity, mistakes, and sin—including our own—and all their
natural consequences. We will face affliction whether we
want to or not, no matter how much our feeble human
hands try to mitigate it. This is the focus of the ninth
stanza of Psalm 119, titled "Teth."

Acting surprised, angry, upset, and shocked when we
face affliction reveals stunning immaturity and foolish-
ness caused by a lack of biblical knowledge. Using our
affliction as a reason to blame God or as an excuse for
unwise actions reveals ignorance of the real genesis of

affliction.

Affliction has its roots in human depravity, going all the way back to Adam and Eve and their sin in the Garden of Eden. Free will also contributes to affliction.

I remember when I was going through pain that drove me into the Word. I poured out my heart to God, and I learned how to use Psalm 142 and Psalm 143. I pray that affliction will always drive me to the Word of God.

—From Joe's journal

When God taught me how Psalm 142 and 143 could comfort me in my affliction, I had been attending college for a few years. I had no idea what would happen years later in the family I didn't even have yet.

At the time, however, the affliction I was going through was rough, and God used it to teach me how to run to His Word in difficult circumstances. I learned that without the Word, affliction will become an excuse to complain, speak poorly of God, and become useless. But a lover of God's Word can embrace these inevitable trials and be comforted and filled with joy as they see God's Word verified.

Remember those six daily prayers from Chapter Five? Remember that prayer asking God to confirm His Word to us? He's much more likely to do that through affliction than through giving you a great job. Make sure you know what you're praying for when you pray those prayers.

Supreme Court Chief Justice John Roberts spoke about the value of affliction in a 2017 commencement address. It was one of the most profound statements on the topic I have ever read, outside of Scripture:

From time to time in the years to come, I hope you will be treated unfairly, so that you will come to know the value of justice. I hope that you will suffer betrayal because that will teach you the importance of loyalty. Sorry to say, but I hope you will be lonely from time to time so that you don't take friends for granted. I wish you bad luck, again, from time to time so that you will be conscious of the role of chance in life and understand that your success is not completely deserved and that the failure of others is not completely deserved either. And when you lose, as you will from time to time, I hope every now and then, your opponent will gloat over your failure. It is a way for you to understand the importance of sportsmanship. I hope you'll be ignored so you know the importance of listening to others, and I hope you will have just enough pain to learn compassion. Whether I wish these things or not, they're going to happen. And whether you benefit from them or not will depend upon your ability to see the message in your misfortunes.[26]

Chief Justice Roberts stumbles upon an amazing truth here: we will never learn spiritual truths without the soil of affliction. Affliction allows God's Word to take root in our hearts. Otherwise, it just resides in our minds as unused information.

To a lover of God's Word, affliction is the light at the end of the tunnel, not the midnight of darkness. It's the road sign guiding us to where and how we should live, the exit ramp off the highway of ignorance.

That's how the psalmist describes it. He begins this stanza by talking about how his life is prosperous, better than it was before. The next six verses focus on affliction and why the psalmist is thankful for it.

Historical: Hebrew Word Study

Let's dig a little deeper into this stanza by exploring some of the original Hebrew. The word translated as "well" in verse 65 is the Hebrew *towb,* which indicates prosperity, contentment, and being comparatively better to before.[27]

The word *afflicted* appears twice in this stanza, in verses 67 and 71. This comes from the Hebrew word *anah,* which means "to be oppressed or humbled, to humble yourself, or to bow down." *Anah* is in turn derived from a root word that means "to answer, respond, or testify or to speak, shout, or declare."[28] In other words, the root word of affliction in this passage is tied to teaching!

We would never understand just how amazing the Word of God is if we didn't take the time to study it. In addition, we would never experience the supernatural power of God's word without affliction. The psalmist unmistakably tied his perspective on affliction to his relationship with God's Word.

Theological: The Value of Affliction

In verse 67, the psalmist sets up the thesis of the entire stanza, "Before I was afflicted, I went astray, but now I keep Your word" (NKJV).

He is essentially saying, "Here's where I am right now, and here's how I got there." The psalmist then describes the value of affliction for a person in tune with God's Word.

1. Affliction changes your direction. The psalmist's wayward path was the source of his affliction. He suffered because of the choices and decisions he made of his own free will. God's Word taught the psalmist why his affliction came about and enabled him to learn lessons that changed his behavior. Affliction allows you to experience God's Word in a transformational way when you ask God to show you the source of your affliction, teach you His ways, and set you on His path.

2. Affliction changes how we view God. Amid

affliction, the psalmist was able to say of God, "You are good, and do good; teach me Your statutes" (v. 68 NKJV).

Our natural response to affliction is to blame God, act defensive, feel justified, judge others, or even seek revenge.

We are tempted to say, "It's just not fair! Why would this happen to me? I don't deserve this." In doing so, we reveal what we think of God's character and person. We reveal that we consider Him a liar and a fraud for allowing our free will to cause us affliction and for not allowing us to be sinful without experiencing consequences. We think of ourselves as victimized by God instead of reliant upon His grace.

As victims, our inevitable afflictions become definite failures and wasted opportunities. But with God's Word, we see God not as the source of affliction but as our Healer, our life raft.

3. *Affliction causes you to fall out of love with the world*: "The proud have forged a lie against me, but I will keep Your precepts with my whole heart. Their heart is as fat as grease, but I delight in Your law" (Psalm 119:69–70 NKJV).

The psalmist is not necessarily talking about specific people; he's referring to the wicked world around him. He was falling out of love with the world because he recognized the world causes affliction.

A deficiency in God's Word blinds our eyes to spiritual things, training our focus on the glitzy things around us, the things of this world. But affliction combined with God's Word helps us see the frailty of this world and gives us motivation to develop a new value system by changing what's important to us.

When my family was going through the grieving process with the loss of our daughter, my pastor at the time, Brian Yost, preached a sermon about not wasting your grief. That sermon has stayed with me. When we are in love with the world more than we love God's Word, we often waste our grief, our affliction.

4. Affliction helps you embrace it rather than fear it: "It is good for me that I have been afflicted, that I may learn Your statutes. The law of Your mouth is better to me than thousands of coins of gold and silver" (Psalm 119:71–72 NKJV).

The difference between being a victor in tough times or being a victim with a "woe is me" mentality is recognizing that affliction will come and those who love God's Word will be motivated to run to truth and Heavenly Dad. The miracle of affliction is that even during it, you can look back and see how it brings you closer to Heavenly Dad than ever before.

God deals well with those who love His Word, those to whom He has given the gift of faith: "You have dealt well with Your servant, O LORD, according to Your word. Teach me good judgment and knowledge, for I believe Your commandments" (Psalm 119:65–66 NKJV).

That is the theme for the six verses that follow, which explain how the psalmist got to the life described in those first two verses. The psalmist did not praise God because his life was perfect, and everything was going his way. He praised God because he had been afflicted and that affliction had transformed his life. Instead of continuing to go astray, the psalmist learned God's statutes through that affliction.

Going through affliction will reveal you are one of two types of people. The first type is described in James 1:2–3: "Count it all joy, my brothers, when you meet trials of various kinds, for you know that the testing of your faith produces steadfastness."

James describes the second type of person a few verses later: "But let him ask in faith, with no doubting, for the one who doubts is like a wave of the sea that is driven and tossed by the wind" (James 1:6).

There are those who respond to affliction steadfastly, like a rock, and those who respond to affliction in a way that is unstable, causing them sway to and fro like an ocean wave. Which type will you be?

Devotional: God Deals Well with Us

God's Word was confirmed to me when I went through that pre-season of affliction in college. Later, I went through the regular season of affliction, followed by some playoff affliction.

When hardships come, and I expect it soon, I will remember I am God's child, and He will deal well with me. I will understand the benefits and purposes of my trials, even if I cannot see the reason these trials have come. I will trust that God is sovereign, and I won't allow affliction to separate me from Him or His Word.
—From Joe's journal

The combination of affliction with God's Word enables me to echo the psalmist and say, "Let me tell you how God deals well with me." As hard as it is for our family each year on the anniversary of my daughter's death, it's also a stark reminder of the goodness of God amid affliction. Just in case you doubt me, by God's sovereign hand, today as I am doing my final edit of this chapter, it's the day of that dark anniversary! Just try and tell me God doesn't love His children! When dealing with adversity and trials, it's a comfort to know my God always deals well with me.

When adversity shows up, we can trust God's love and concern for our welfare. We may not always understand on this side of heaven exactly why or how things can be well with us, but the Word of God allows us to understand and believe He deals well with us.

All this is rooted in the fact that God is good. Affliction enables us to see His goodness more clearly.

> *Who shall separate us from the love of Christ? Shall tribulation, or distress, or persecution, or famine, or nakedness, or danger, or sword? As it is written, "For your sake we are being killed all the day long; we are regarded as sheep to be slaughtered." No, in all these things we are more than conquerors through him who loved us. For I am sure that neither death nor life, nor angels nor rulers, nor things present nor things to come, nor powers, nor height nor depth, nor anything else in all creation, will be able to separate us from the love of God in Christ Jesus our Lord.*
> *—Romans 8:35–39*

Why is this? Because God does well by us. Even during our suffering, whether it's brought on by our depravity, the world's depravity, our unwise decisions, or malicious decisions of others—all of which we sometimes try to blame on God—God will do well by us.

Loving God's Word will enable you to see, declare, and sing that God deals well with you, no matter what.

WORKBOOK

Chapter Nine Questions

Question: Think back to two or three seasons of affliction you have been through in your life. Were you consistently connected to God's Word throughout this time? if so, how did it help you through your suffering? And if not, how might Scripture have changed your perspective and made your difficulties more endurable?

_____

_____

_____

_____

_____

_____

_____

_____

_____

_____

Question: How has affliction, coupled with God's Word, changed your direction, your view of God, your attitude toward the world, and your response to suffering itself?

_____

_____

_____

_____

_____

_____

_____

_____

_____

Question: Give examples from the Bible and/or your own life of God's goodness amid suffering and affliction. Even during a tragedy, how can you see God dealing well with His people?

_____

_____

_____

_____

_____

_____

_____

_____

_____

_____

_____

_____

Action: Read the story behind the beloved Christian hymn "It is Well" by Horatio G. Spafford and sing or listen to a recording of this song, considering the words in light of the affliction that the author endured.

Chapter Nine Notes

CHAPTER TEN

Yodh—Redemption Makeover

A makeup kit is a great picture of how we as Christians tend to approach religion. We do many religious things in hopes of giving ourselves a spiritual makeover. We desperately want to be transformed and be better than we are right now, so we seek all kinds of advice.

We want the quickest, most efficient makeover possible, and so we equip ourselves with all kinds of tools we can use to change our outward appearance to that of a good churchgoer. But without a daily infusion of God's Word, we're only fixing our hair, covering up our spiritual blemishes.

That's not real change. It's just religious makeup that doesn't alter who we are inside.

Before I started studying the Word of God for myself, I was the epitome of a lack of confidence in God. I had a quick temper, unhealthy relationships, and constant shame. I know this is all new right now, but I can already see where God's Word is changing me and making me a completely new person and pastor.

—From Joe's journal

In this stanza, titled "Yodh," the psalmist explains how God's Word gave him a complete makeover that started with the dynamic power of redemption.

*Your hands have **made** me and **fashioned** me; give me understanding, that I may learn Your commandments. Those who fear You will **be glad** when they see me, because I have hoped in Your word. I know, O LORD, that Your judgments are right, and that in faithfulness You have afflicted me. Let, I pray, Your merciful kindness be for my comfort, according to Your word to Your servant. Let Your tender mercies come to me, that I may live; for Your law is my delight. Let the proud be ashamed, for they treated me wrongfully with falsehood; but I will meditate on Your precepts. Let those who fear You turn to me, those who know Your testimonies. Let my heart be blameless regarding Your statutes, that I may not be ashamed.*
—***Psalm 119:73–80*** *(NKJV)*

Historical: Hebrew Word Study

Let's dig into some of the original Hebrew of this passage. The word translated as "made" in verse 73 is the Hebrew word *asah*, which means "to work or trim, as with gold or silver."[29] Isn't that a beautiful picture?

The word "fashioned," which is also in verse 73, is the Hebrew *kuwn*, meaning "to be fitted or tailored, to shape or reform."[30] The psalmist is essentially saying God's hands dressed him in gold and silver and set him upright. God's truth has shaped and reformed him.

Lastly, we have the phrase "be glad" in verse 74, which is the Hebrew word *samach*. The ESV translates this same phrase as "rejoice." This word means "to brighten up, cheer up, to make joyful, to give cause for rejoicing."[31] This concept of a spiritual makeover and the joy it brings is repeated throughout Scripture, as we see here:

I will greatly rejoice in the LORD, my soul shall be joyful in
my God; for He has clothed me with the garments of salva-
tion, He has covered me with the robe of righteousness, as
a bridegroom decks himself with ornaments, and as a bride
adorns herself with her jewels.
—*Isaiah 61:10 (NKJV)*

God gives us this image because He knows we are focused on the outward. He shows us that the righteousness
and other qualities He is giving us on the inside—in our
hearts—are comparable to the outer adornments we think
of when we think of a makeover. He is reshaping us and
giving us a tailor-made suit of clothing for our justification and redemption.

As you can see, redemption is a very important topic
when it comes to being made over and transformed spiritually. God's Word is the only place we can go to learn
about redemption.

Theological: How God Changes Us Through a Redemption Makeover

The next six verses of this stanza explain how God
makes over our lives, dressing us up in righteousness. A
redemption makeover is not limited to the following
changes, but these are the changes the psalmist points out
in this passage.

1. God changes our confidence: "I know, O LORD, that
Your judgments are right, and that in faithfulness You
have afflicted me. Let, I pray, Your merciful kindness be
for my comfort, according to Your word to Your servant.
Let Your tender mercies come to me, that I may live; for
Your law is my delight" (Psalm 119:75–77 NKJV).

This goes back to our prayer list in Chapter Five, in
which we asked God to confirm His Word to us and make
us know it's true. Here, the psalmist is acknowledging

God did this for him.

If we don't spend time in God's Word, we have no reason to have confidence in truth because we don't know enough about truth. We turn our trust to things that will feed our thirst for emotional satisfaction rather than spiritual satisfaction. Put simply, without God's Word we trust our feeling more than we trust our God, because we have no confidence in our experience with His Word.

How can we know anything about redemption if we've never read the expert source on the subject? We spend so much time analyzing how we feel, why we feel that way, and whose fault it is. We are driven by circumstances, searching for favorable conditions we can trust and have confidence in.

The psalmist, however, prayed that God's mercy would be his comfort and his confidence, for God's Word had become His delight.

As God's Word is confirmed to you, your confidence in truth begins to grow exponentially: "And I am sure of this, that he who began a good work in you will bring it to completion at the day of Jesus Christ" (Philippians 1:6).

You realize God's Word and what it has to say about redemption is worthy of your confidence, your trust. I can promise you with as much integrity as I can muster that this is not theory. I've lived it.

2. God changes our temper and our anger: "Let the proud be ashamed, for they treated me wrongfully with falsehood; but I will meditate on Your precepts" (Psalm 119:78 NKJV).

If left unchecked, anger, resentment, bitterness, and frustration will consume your life and define how others see you. However, when you have a redemptive makeover, anger becomes less of a dominating factor in your life.

We don't have to look far to find a reason to be frustrated or upset. When we are habitually angry, frustrated, bitter, or resentful, it stunts our growth. It's impossible to grow when anger is dominating your life. It's the downfall of many believers and why many Christians never grow.

The psalmist acknowledged that people had done a lot of things that he should be upset about, but he chose not to dwell on them. Instead, he chose to fill His mind with God's Word, which enabled him to escape bitterness and anger. Even though the psalmist naturally wanted to be angry, he could trust God's truth and let God deal with the people who hurt him. Bitterness cannot live for long in a heart filled with God's Word and His truth.

We tend to get angry and then run to God's Word for relief, like we would run to the medicine cabinet for an aspirin. That's not how it works—we need to fill our hearts with God's Word *before* we get angry. When we are filled with truth, we won't be vulnerable to fits of rage and bitterness when people wrong us. A heart that's empty of God's Word is a heart that will respond in anger.

James 1:19–20 tells us: "Know this, my beloved brothers: let every person be quick to hear, slow to speak, slow to anger; for the anger of man does not produce the righteousness of God."

Somehow, we have convinced ourselves that if we communicate our anger effectively enough, the person who wronged us will apologize, even change their behavior. But wrath is not a catalyst for positive change. As God's Word becomes more of a part of your life, anger becomes less of a part of it.

3. God changes our relationships: "Let those who fear You turn to me, those who know Your testimonies" (Psalm 119:79 NKJV).

We become surrounded by relationships founded upon a common love of God's Word.

A person without God's Word has very little ability to cultivate healthy, God-centered relationships. Many people choose relationships based upon human criteria or worldly standards and then become captive to those relationships emotionally, spiritually, and physically. They become codependent and destructive relationships. If you happen to stumble upon a good relationship without a consistent connection to God's Word, it's pure grace.

The psalmist trusted God's Word to set the standards for his relationships. Doing this will save you a world of trouble. As the Word of God becomes a daily part of your heart and life, God gives you a desire to connect with people who live by those same standards. As Paul warned the Corinthians, "Do not be deceived: 'Bad company ruins good morals'" (1 Corinthians 15:33).

4. God changes our shame: "Let my heart be blameless regarding Your statutes, that I may not be ashamed" (Psalm 119:80 NKJV).

God takes us out of the prison of guilt and shame and transfers us to a life of running in a wide place of mercy.

Shame is a powerful force in our lives. It's the result of not understanding grace and redemption. The only reason a Christian can feel shame is because they don't understand those concepts, and only God's Word will provide that understanding.

Grace and redemption are ridiculous, illogical, and miraculous. Though we are sinners who have offended our most holy God, He has chosen to save us rather than give us the punishment our sins deserve. But it goes beyond salvation. As we spend time in God's Word, He will also save us from the prison of shame.

This is the part about Christianity most people don't understand. Feeling guilty does not make you guilty. Either you're guilty or you're not, regardless of how you feel. Some people don't feel guilty, yet they are. You must learn to live in the reality of forgiveness through Christ, not in the feelings of guilt and shame.

This is not a license for sin.

What shall we say then? Are we to continue in sin that grace may abound? By no means! How can we who died to sin still live in it? Do you not know that all of us who have been baptized into Christ Jesus were baptized into his death? We were buried therefore with him by baptism into death, in order that, just as Christ was raised from the dead by the glory of the Father, we too might walk in newness of life.

—Romans 6:1–4

This doesn't mean we're perfect. As God works a redemption makeover in our lives, we recognize we are sinners and have deficiencies and shortcomings, but we also know we don't have to live with shame. That is the concept of escaping the prison of shame and recognizing the reality of forgiveness.

It's unmistakable when God's Word begins this redemption makeover, this process of transformation. My friend Mark Curtis runs all-day seminars on the twelve steps of recovery that numerous people attend. The Mark I knew five years ago would not have been spending six hours on a Saturday with these people, but God has transformed him. He is an example of someone who has confidence in God's Word. His relationships are changing, and he's escaping the prison of shame as he develops confidence in God's forgiveness in his own life. It's amazing.

Devotional: Freedom Through Redemption

Next to the moment of salvation, the most exciting time for a Christ-follower is when it dawns on you that God is working the miracle of redemption in your life. You recognize redemption and God's Word are transforming you, and it's exciting.

God's Word takes a life that's tattered, dilapidated, frazzled, unkempt, unstable, bitter, angry, and burned to the ground and transforms it into a shimmering fashion statement about the power of redemption. Adorning us with the gold and silver of mercy and grace, fitting us with robes of righteousness that help us escape the prison of shame, God's Word takes sinful, fallen, unstable, angry, bitter, selfish, world-loving people and transforms us step by step.

> Now the Lord is the Spirit, and where the Spirit of the Lord is, there is freedom. And we all, with unveiled face, beholding the glory of the Lord, are being transformed into the same image from one degree of glory to another. For this comes from the Lord who is the Spirit.
> —*2 Corinthians 3:17–18*

What is the glory of the Lord that we're witnessing? It's Him changing us. The more you learn about redemption, the more evident the makeover becomes. It's not just forgiveness, it's transformation.

Are you tired of hoping you'll one day be the Christ-follower you should be? I can tell you why you're struggling: you're not in love with God's Word. You will need to learn more about what redemption does, and there's only one place for that—His Word.

The psalmist recognized the Word of God was changing him, that God had made him, dressed him in gold and silver, and outfitted him in specially tailored clothes of righteousness. God gives us a new nature. We don't have to be held captive to our old nature anymore because we're in love with God through His Word, and we love to read it every day.

WORKBOOK

Chapter Ten Questions

Question: What are some ways you have tried to fix or makeover your Christian image? What is your motivation for wanting to have this perfect outer image, and how does focusing on the outward sometimes obscure the real issues on the inside?

_____

_____

_____

_____

_____

_____

_____

_____

_____

_____

Question: You have to learn to live in the reality of forgiveness through Christ, not in the feelings of guilt and shame. How can you allow the Word and the reality of Christ's forgiveness to overcome the strong emotional pull of guilt and shame? When you are regularly facing the ongoing consequences of a past sin or mistake, how practically can you still walk in the freedom of grace?

_____

_____

_____

_____

_____

_____

_____

_____

_____

_____

_____

Question: What are some ways you can see God at work in changing and redeeming you? How are you different now than you were six months ago, a year, two years? What further work could God do in transforming you if you had more exposure to His Word, a deeper understand of redemption?

_____

_____

_____

_____

_____

_____

_____

_____

_____

_____

_____

_____

Action: Make a list of some key verses about anger and wrath. Write or type these out and work on memorizing one each week. Allow God's Word to transform your natural bent toward anger and to help you instead respond redemptively to frustrating people and situations.

_____

_____

_____

_____

_____

_____

_____

_____

Chapter Ten Notes

CHAPTER ELEVEN

Kaph—Eyes on Eternity

If salvation and the Word of God are so important to us as Christians, then why do we struggle with obsession with the present? The reason is for most people, eternity and God's Word aren't that important. Our lives and our focus say the present is far more significant than eternity. It's an understandable struggle, since *now* is right in our face.

The world and eternity are constantly battling each other for our hearts. The world is constantly drawing our focus away from eternity and salvation. It draws our attention to what it has to offer us, claiming eternity is too far away, something we don't really need to think about right now.

Frankly, unless God's Word is a crucial part of your everyday life, you have no motivation to trust in eternity because you won't know anything about it. Where else will you learn about eternal promises except from God's Word? If His Word isn't part of your life, all you will hear are the world's promises, and that is what you will pursue day after day.

146 · JOSEPH DAVIS

I remember being betrayed to the greatest level by a friend in college. Those questions of why, how long, and many others haunted me for several weeks. In the end however, it was crystal clear what God was doing. I needed some things removed from my life before He could use me. I clung to the promises in God's Word, while at the same time, questioning God. God did not answer those questions immediately. That time of affliction was one of the lowest points in my life. However, in the end, God proved to be faithful to His Word.

—From Joe's Journal

Without clinging to God's Word, any talk of eternity is just a religious show. It's lip service because our trust and our hope are for a better life here and now, not reliant upon God's eternal promises. Without God's Word, your trust, confidence, and attention will remain focused on your desire for worldly things, not the wow things in God's Word.

You will be focused more on your opinion of justice than on God's justice. You will desire the world's love instead of God's love and the love of His people. Why do I say that? Because Christian fellowship, our love for each other, is a wonderful *now* preview of eternity.

In the eleventh stanza of Psalm 119, titled "Kaph," the psalmist describes his longings and how they affect his focus here on earth.

*My soul **faints** for Your **salvation**, but I hope in Your word. My eyes fail from searching **Your word**, saying, "When will You comfort me?" For I have become like a wineskin in smoke, yet I do not forget Your statutes. How many are the days of Your servant? When will You execute judgment on those who persecute me? The proud have dug pits for me, which is not according to Your law. All Your commandments are faithful; they persecute me wrongfully; help me! They almost made an end of me on earth, but I did not*

forsake Your precepts. Revive me according to Your loving-kindness, so that I may keep the testimony of Your mouth.
—**Psalm 119:81–88** *(NKJV, emphasis added)*

Historical: Hebrew Word Study

Let's look at the Hebrew words the psalmist uses for the things he longs for. In verse 81, the Hebrew word translated as "faints" is *kalah*, which means "to end, cease, finish, complete or accomplish, to bring to pass."[32] The psalmist longed to look past the present and see all the benefits of the culmination, the finished product.

Also in verse 81, the word "salvation" is the Hebrew word *teshuah*, meaning "deliverance or salvation."[33] The psalmist desired the completion of his salvation. His heart was burdened with the desire to be completely and finally delivered to experience eternal victory.

Lastly, the Hebrew word translated as "Your word" in verse 82 is the Hebrew word *imrah,* which means "commandment."[34] In this context, it refers to the Word of God or the Torah, which is the first five books of the Old Testament. The psalmist equated salvation with God's Word. "So faith comes from hearing, and hearing through the word of Christ" (Romans 10:17). The psalmist makes a clear distinction that since he was thinking about salvation, eternity, and heaven, he was therefore thinking about God's Word.

Because the poetry of the psalmist describes salvation as being synonymous with the Word of God, he knew his salvation, the promise, was the Word of God, the gospel—not religion or human effort or the world around him.

God's Word enabled him to see the day of judgment in the same light as salvation. Think about that for a minute. We tend to think of judgment day as bad and the day of salvation as good. But the psalmist says they're the same day! If you're a child of God, judgment day is salvation day, the day when Jesus declares you are clean, pure, and righteous and you belong to Him.

The psalmist could express his longing for salvation and for God to judge those who tried to trap him because he saw both days as the same. His hope for eternity was founded in and fueled by his connection to God's Word.

Theological: The Word of God Transforms Our Yearnings

God's Word causes us to yearn for several things.

1. God's Word causes us to long for salvation: "My soul faints for Your salvation, but I hope in Your word. My eyes fail from searching Your word, saying, 'When will You comfort me?' For I have become like a wineskin in smoke, yet I do not forget Your statutes" (Psalm 119:81–83 NKJV).

The psalmist's soul—his spirit man—longed for God's salvation. The Word of God made his eyes—his physical man—long for salvation as well. Both his spirit man and his physical man longed for heaven—eternity—and for God's Word.

He compares himself to a wineskin being cracked and dried out by smoke. Even though death was working in his physical man—the wineskin—the psalmist knew his spirit man—the wine—would not be wasted because he had confidence God had made him a new creation. He knew he would eventually be a new wineskin.

God's Word enables us to cling to the hope of a new wineskin. That's where salvation lies. We are new creatures. The old things have passed away, and all things have become new (2 Corinthians 5:17). Theologically, that's what God's Word will do for you. It will make you long for salvation, and the new creation it's making you.

2. God's Word causes us to long for His judgment, not

ours: "How many are the days of Your servant? When will You execute judgment on those who persecute me? The proud have dug pits for me, which is not according to Your law. All Your commandments are faithful; they persecute me wrongfully; help me!" (Psalm 119:84–86 NKJV).

Nothing will force obsession with the world around us more than being wronged or betrayed. That's when it's hard to have faith, when the temptation to take matters into your own hands can be overwhelming. But taking matters into your own hands is, by definition, obsession with the now.

By doing so, you basically declare you do not trust the day of judgment—therefore you do not trust the day of salvation. You are setting yourself up as judge. Scary, isn't it?

The questions the psalmist asks—"When will You comfort me?" (v. 82), "How much longer is this going to go on?" (v. 84), "When will You judge those who persecute me?" (v. 84)—do not mean he's struggling with faith. These are questions about redemption, about how difficult it was to wait as the world continued to dry him out. He was obsessed with the hardships he experienced and wanted to know when his salvation would be complete.

The psalmist's questions were pointed toward the day of salvation, toward eternity, when he would finally see God face to face. It's okay for us to ask these questions too, and express grief over what we're experiencing right now in this hard world. It's called crying out to God.

David and Job both asked these questions and made similar petitions. The key is they did not forsake their trust in God's Word. If we have that connection with God's Word, we no longer fear His judgment, knowing we are safe from it and will receive redemption and grace. Instead, God's Word enables us in some miraculous, ridiculous way to look forward to judgment!

We all have sin in our lives. But when you understand redemption and grace and understand what God's Word does for you, you know that as bad as you are, judgment day isn't going to be a problem! The idea of judgment day becomes a comfort! We know in Christ, we will be found blameless. That's a supernatural mindset you can only get from spending time in God's Word.

3. *God's Word causes us to long for an earthly connection to the Father.* You will know God's Word is really changing your heart when you begin to forsake the allure of the now connection with the world for a connection with Eternal Dad. Your eyes become fixed on salvation: "They almost made an end of me on earth, but I did not forsake Your precepts. Revive me according to Your lovingkindness, so that I may keep the testimony of Your mouth" (Psalm 119:87–88 NKJV).

No matter what your earthly circumstances, you maintain this connection to the Father as the most important thing to you. You recognize this connection with Heavenly Dad is your source of life, hope, and sustainability.

The world around you, while loud and obnoxious, becomes nothing more than a pesky mosquito when you have an eternal perspective and are awaiting the day of salvation. It can be a big, painful mosquito at times— maybe even a wasp—but you know that as pesky and painful as this life can be, the end of your salvation is coming. You are therefore able to live life with eyes focused on salvation.

But we have this treasure in jars of clay, to show that the surpassing power belongs to God and not to us. We are afflicted in every way, but not crushed; perplexed, but not driven to despair; persecuted, but not forsaken; struck down, but not destroyed; always carrying in the body the death of Jesus, so that the life of Jesus may also be manifested in our bodies. For we who live are always being

*given over to death for Jesus' sake, so that the life of Jesus
also may be manifested in our mortal flesh. So death is at
work in us, but life in you.*

*So we do not lose heart. Though our outer self is wasting
away, our inner self is being renewed day by day. For this
light momentary affliction is preparing for us an eternal
weight of glory beyond all comparison, as we look not to
the things that are seen but to the things that are unseen.
For the things that are seen are transient, but the things
that are unseen are eternal.*
—2 Corinthians 4:7–12, 16–18

The present is nothing compared to eternity. God's
Word frees us from obsession with the present so we can
long for salvation. That's hard to do when all you can
think of is right now.

Can you see how a life lived with awareness of eternity
can be much more effective in this temporary world? The
values and wisdom that drive your daily decisions will be
starkly different when you have eyes for eternity. The
Word of God enables you to see the folly of obsession
with the moment and to embrace living for heaven.

Longing for the world's things and even the world's
justice will leave us heartbroken and gasping for air, but a
relationship with God's Word frees us from the burden of
right now. It gives us a secret weapon in the constant battle between the present and eternity. It enables us to have
a supernatural desire for eternity and salvation.

That's what spending time in God's Word does. It flips
your longings 180 degrees toward salvation and eternity,
God's judgment, and earthly connection to Heavenly Dad.

Devotional: How Eternity Impacts the Present

How can you tell if eternity is impacting you and if

you're spending enough time in God's Word? Take some time to reflect on the following questions:

1. What do you spend your money on?
2. What do you spend your time on?
3. What brand of judgment are you looking for—yours or God's?
4. How much are you drawn to truth?

"Whoever seeks to preserve his life will lose it, but whoever loses his life will keep it" (Luke 17:33 ESV). It's impossible to understand Luke 17:33 without having a relationship with God's Word. Once that has become a priority in your life, you'll have the ability to look ahead. The less you feel the urge to hold on to the present, the more you're able to grasp and hold on to eternity, which is only possible through a consistent relationship with God's Word.

You can tell if you are thinking about eternity by how you spend your money and your time, your brand of judgment, and whether you long for truth.

As God's Word is confirmed in your life, you will see its impact on your eternal perspective. You begin to long for the final outcomes of redemption. Remember that prayer list from Chapter Five:

- "Teach me, God. It won't be a waste."

- "God, make me obey Your Word. When I do, my life is so much better."

- "God, make it natural for me to love Your Word more than temporary stuff."

- "Confirm the power of Your Word to me, Lord. It excites and motivates me."

- "Protect me from my own sinful ways. I hate them, but I know Your Word is good."
- "Make me excited and alive concerning Your righteousness."

When you start focusing on eternity, you have a better understanding of what life is for. If life is just for the present, it's nothing more than a constant battle, and any wins are temporary. Through Christ, however, we have an ultimate victory to look forward to—a complete and total blowout that cannot be contested or overturned.

We need to learn to focus on that victory, but to do that, we need to spend time in God's Word. Like the psalmist, we need to long for God's Word, because His Word is our salvation.

WORKBOOK

Chapter Eleven Questions

Question: What are some temporal or worldly things, good or bad, that keep you from staying focused on eternity? What are your greatest longings and what is their eternal significance? Is it harder for you to keep an eternal perspective when things are going well or when you are facing difficulties?

_____

_____

_____

_____

_____

_____

_____

_____

_____

Question: What are some hard questions that you have wrestled with or asked God about? Where do you see injustices and innocent people suffering? How will the day of salvation/judgment make these unresolved things right?

_____

_____

_____

_____

_____

_____

_____

_____

_____

_____

Question: A relationship with God's Word gives you a secret weapon in the constant battle between the present and eternity. What are some passages from the Bible that help you to find and keep an eternal perspective during present pressures?

_____

_____

_____

_____

_____

_____

_____

_____

_____

_____

_____

_____

Action: For a week or so, take notes on your use of time and money. Then review, noting how much of each commodity is eternity-focused and how much is temporal-focused. Where will you make changes to practically live with eternity in view?

_____

_____

_____

_____

_____

_____

_____

_____

_____

_____

Chapter Eleven Notes

_____

_____

_____

_____

_____

_____

_____

_____

_____

_____

_____

_____

_____

_____

_____

_____

_____

_____

_____

_____

CHAPTER TWELVE

Lamedh—Forever Satisfying

After a while, my Boston CDs, tacos, sports, science, family, friends, cars, even ministry fails to satisfy. But God's Word never ceases to amaze me, challenge me, intimidate me, comfort me, transform me, and satisfy me. It is roomy in any and every direction. It is without limitation in its content, its wisdom, power, influence, and durability. It is exceedingly broad. Everything on this earth I hold dear will fail me and be consumed sooner or later. That will not and cannot happen with the Word of God.

—From Joe's journal

It's amazing how easily we fall for the lie of satisfaction from the world—its people, its pursuits, its possessions. We expect them to fill us and give us purpose, and we'll chase after them in hopes we'll somehow, someday, finally get enough.

But that's the great lie: these things never last and ultimately force you to go further than you want to go. "They'll make you stay longer than you want to stay and cost you more than you're ever willing to pay."[35]

The world gets old fast. Even the things you enjoy the most will ultimately make you sick or bored. They lose their shine because the world wasn't made to endure forever. But the miracle of God's Word is that those who really love it never grow tired of reading it, studying it, or talking about it. It's always fresh and new, always powerful, always challenging, and always fascinating.

This is exactly what the psalmist is looking to convey in the twelfth stanza, which is titled "Lamedh." It's the dead center of Psalm 119, and it's constructed slightly differently than the other stanzas. It's set up like a song.

1. First, we have verses 89–91: "Forever, O LORD, Your word is settled in heaven. Your faithfulness endures to all generations; You established the earth, and it abides. They continue this day according to Your ordinances, for all are Your servants" (NKJV).

This is the hook, the chorus that sticks in your mind and deserves to be repeated over and over. There are a lot of catchy choruses in this world, but all of them get a bit old after a while. This chorus, however, is the core of this whole album of songs we call Psalm 119. It beautifully and memorably encapsulates the reason the psalmist was inspired to create the greatest artistic expression of God's Word in human history.

2. The second part of the song is verses 92–96: "Unless Your law had been my delight, I would then have perished in my affliction. I will never forget Your precepts, for by them You have given me life. I am Yours, save me; for I have sought Your precepts. The wicked wait for me to destroy me, but I will consider Your testimonies. I have seen the consummation of all perfection, but Your commandment is exceedingly broad" (NKJV).

This is the verse that would be sandwiched in between repetitions of the chorus. It's constructed so that you would sing verses 89–91, then verses 92–96, and then verses 89–91. That word "broad" in verse 96, by the way, is the same word we studied in Chapter Six, where we learned about the wide place.[36] That's been an important theme throughout the psalm.

As in any good song, the verse gives you more information and greater understanding about the story the song is telling. The repeated chorus is all about giving you a good summary of what the artist is trying to communicate.

As we dig into the original Hebrew of this passage, I want you to understand something very important. Biblically speaking, God's Word is the same as the Word, our Lord and Savior Jesus Christ. What the psalmist is saying about God's Word is therefore also true of Jesus.

When we decide we aren't going to spend time in God's Word, we are basically saying we don't want to spend time with Jesus. Conversely, spending time in God's Word and growing in our love for it means we are also spending time with Jesus and growing in our love for Him. At this halfway point in Psalm 119, let's be mindful that Jesus and the Word of God are one and the same and resist the temptation to set Jesus aside for the sake of our love for the world.

Historical: Hebrew Word Study

Forever, O LORD, Your word is settled in **heaven.** *Your faithfulness endures to* **all generations;** *You established the earth, and it* **abides.** *They continue this day according to Your ordinances, for all are Your servants. Unless Your law had been my delight, I would then have perished in my affliction. I will never forget Your precepts, for by them You have given me life. I am Yours, save me; for I have sought Your precepts. The wicked wait for me to destroy me, but I will consider Your testimonies. I have seen the consummation of all perfection, but Your commandment is exceedingly broad.*
—**Psalm 119:89–96** *(NKJV, emphasis added)*

1. The first concept the psalmist communicates is the limitless nature of the Word of God. The word translated as "heaven" in verse 89 is the Hebrew *shamayim*, which refers to the visible arc of the sky in which the clouds move, even where the planets revolve.[37]

The psalmist is saying the Word of God is just as real and foundational as the existence of the universe around us. Isn't that an amazing picture? It brings to mind a concept that Paul expresses:

> *For by him all things were created, in heaven and on earth, visible and invisible, whether thrones or dominions or rulers or authorities—all things were created through him and for him. And he is before all things, and in him all things hold together.*
> *—Colossians 1:16–17*

These verses in Colossians lead to another truth that will help you understand why God's Word is so expansive. That's included in our next Hebrew word.

2. The second concept the psalmist communicates is the timelessness of the Word of God. The Hebrew word translated "all generations" in verse 90 is *dor*, which refers to an age or generation or the revolution of time. It can also mean eternal.[38]

> *In the beginning was the Word, and the Word was with God, and the Word was God. He was in the beginning with God. All things were made through him, and without him was not any thing made that was made. In him was life, and the life was the light of men.*
> *—John 1:1–4*

The Word of God is considered the light. Remember how in the previous chapter we learned God's Word is salvation and the psalmist longed to see salvation with his eyes? Those verses from the Gospel of John explain the Word of God existed from the very beginning, just as Jesus did. Jesus is the Word become flesh.

And the Word became flesh and dwelt among us, and we have seen his glory, glory as of the only Son from the Father, full of grace and truth.
—John 1:14

And what is truth? God's word is truth (John 17:17). Can you see the picture being painted here? The Word of God is limitless and boundless to all generations because the Word of God is Jesus and Jesus is the Word of God. Scripture teaches us the Word existed from the beginning and Jesus became the Word of God in the flesh and dwelt among us.

3. The third concept the psalmist communicates is the unchanging nature of the Word of God. The Hebrew word translated as "abides" in verse 90 is *amad*, which means "to stand in various relationships, to abide, to confirm, or to continue, endure, establish, or remain."[39] God and His Word endure, as reflected in His enduring creation and in the words of the author of Hebrews: "Jesus Christ is the same yesterday and today and forever" (Hebrews 13:8).

Jesus is God's Word in the flesh. That is why God's Word and Jesus are our salvation. It is an undeniable concept woven throughout Scripture. When the psalmist expressed his longing for God's salvation and his desire to see it with his eyes (vv. 81–82), he was talking about Jesus, the Promised One.

Jesus' own words in the book of Revelation explain both His eternal nature and His role as the key to life:

When I saw him, I fell at his feet as though dead. But he laid his

right hand on me, saying, "Fear not, I am the first and the last,
and the living one. I died, and behold I am alive forevermore,
and I have the keys of Death and Hades."
—Revelation 1:17–18

The Word became flesh, and He is our salvation. He is
the key to eternal satisfaction.

Theological: The Satisfying Word of God

Now that we understand the chorus of the stanza says
what the Word of God is, let's dig into the verse of the
stanza and see how it describes what the Word of God
does.

The psalmist explains three ways God's Word satisfies
us through its truth and through its embodiment in Jesus:

1. God's Word satisfies us emotionally: "Unless Your
law had been my delight, I would then have perished in
my affliction" (Psalm 119:92 NKJV).

The Hebrew word translated as "delight" is *shashua,*
which refers to an enjoyment or pleasure.[40] The psalmist
considered God's law to be his enjoyment.

2. God's Word satisfies us tangibly. Tangible means
we can perceive something by touch or identify it with our
minds. We can understand the thing's value because we
have experienced it physically or mentally.

I will never forget Your precepts, for by them You have
given me life. I am Yours, save me; for I have sought Your
precepts. The wicked wait for me to destroy me, but I will
consider Your testimonies.
—Psalm 119:93–95 *(NKJV)*

The word translated as "consider" is the Hebrew word
biyn, which means "to distinguish mentally, understand,

or feel."[41] You gain understanding by knowing from experience that something is important.

The psalmist was able to assign a value to God's Word because he experienced God confirming His Word in his life. He was physically and mentally satisfied by God's Word because experience taught him how incredible it was.

3. *God's Word satisfies us intellectually*: "I have seen the consummation of all perfection, but your commandment is exceedingly broad" (Psalm 119:96 NKJV).

As we've seen previously in this psalm, the word translated as "broad" is *rachab*, which means "wide and roomy in any or every direction."[42] The truths and insights of God's Word are never exhausted. We can never know all it says.

We are tempted to rely on our achievements, wisdom, understanding, and experiences or those of people we admire. We try to live vicariously through other people and find our purpose and direction in them. But all these have two things in common: their imperfection and their finiteness. What a tremendous comfort to know the Word of God existed from the beginning in the form of Jesus!

Devotional: The World Fails, the Word Won't

The world is constantly trying to trick us with the bait and switch. Merriam-Webster defines bait and switch as "the ploy of offering a person something desirable to gain favor ... then thwarting expectations with something less desirable."[43]

Here's a concrete example. Say someone offers to give you a new name-brand watch, but instead of giving you that, they give you a knockoff that doesn't even work properly. That's a bait and switch. Instead of getting the genuine article you were promised, you get a cheaper version or a counterfeit.

The world promises it will satisfy us, but the satisfaction it offers is a cheap, temporary, counterfeit version of the eternal satisfaction God's Word offers. This is the constant struggle and the war that rages within each child of God. By the gift of faith, however, we see Jesus and God's Word as the same, and suddenly, our passions change.

God's Word, in written form and in the form of Jesus Christ, is eternal salvation. The world is nothing more than one bait and switch after another.

Sam Storms, the lead pastor of Bridgeway Church, in Oklahoma City, Oklahoma, has this to say about the unsurpassed value of God's Word and the satisfaction it provides:

> God's Word is exquisite, sublime, splendid, and sweet. God's Word is powerful, faithful, righteous, and true. God's Word is great, glorious, grand, and good. Why? Because in it we see **God**! Through it, he draws near! By means of its truth, we experience the incomparable joy of knowing **him** and seeing **him** and beholding the beauty of **his** infinite elegance.[44]

God's Word is eternally satisfying because it is our Lord and Savior Jesus Christ, who died on the cross, conquered the grave, rose to life, and is coming again. But here's the problem: we say we want to know Jesus, but we spend very little time with Him—literally with Him, in His Word.

> *In the beginning was the Word, and the Word was with God, and the Word was God. ... And the Word became flesh and dwelt among us, and we have seen his glory, glory as of the only Son from the Father, full of grace and truth.*
> **—John 1:1, 14**

Not only does the Word of God satisfy us day by day, but it also saves us for all eternity. If you truly want to know Jesus, here He is. He's in the pages of your Bible or the megabytes of your Bible app.

Through the LORD's mercies we are not consumed, because His compassions fail not. They are new every morning; Great is Your faithfulness. "The LORD is my portion," says my soul, "Therefore I hope in Him!"
—Lamentations 3:22–24 *(NKJV)*

Do you believe Lamentations? Do you believe God's mercies and His Word and that His salvation is new and fresh every day? Here's the challenge: if you're a child of God, it's time to stop pretending. If you really love Jesus, I've told you where you can see Him and how you can spend time with Him. Don't pretend you love Jesus and then not spend any time with Him.

The psalmist longed to see God's salvation (v. 81). It's in those pages, or those megabytes, that we find it.

WORKBOOK

Chapter Twelve Questions

Question: What are some things you have looked to for satisfaction only to be disappointed over time? How far have you gone in demanding satisfaction from these temporal things, and what has been the result? How can disillusionment ultimately be a blessing?

_____

_____

_____

_____

_____

_____

_____

_____

_____

_____

Question: How can the approach that you are *meeting with Jesus* instead of merely reading a book change your view of Bible reading/study? What are some of the shared attributes of God's Word—the Bible—and the Word made Flesh—Jesus Christ?

_____

_____

_____

_____

_____

_____

_____

_____

_____

_____

Question: What are some areas of your life where you feel unsatisfied? How can a deeper relationship with God's Word (both the Bible and Jesus) meet you in those places of dissatisfaction and transform your thinking and your desires? What does this look like on a practical, daily level when you are dealing with broken relationships, dead-end jobs, financial hardship, or health problems? How does the Word offer you satisfaction that can transcend earthly unhappiness?

_____

_____

_____

_____

_____

_____

_____

_____

_____

_____

Action: Don't pretend you love Jesus and then not spend any time with Him. What does time with Jesus look like for you? How can you spend *more* time and *deeper* time in this current season of your life? What Bible study tools (e.g., devotional book, journal, Bible Study references, worship music) would enhance, but not clutter, this time? Spend some time planning for your times with the Word as diligently as you would prepare for a getaway weekend with someone you love—and then implement your plan.

_____

_____

_____

_____

_____

Chapter Twelve Notes

CHAPTER THIRTEEN

Mem—Eating All Day

The thirteenth stanza of Psalm 119, titled "Mem," is all about meditation. This is not Eastern meditation, which has been corrupted, but true meditation according to Scripture.

Meditation frightens me. I have a long way to go before I can truly say I love God's Word all day. How do I make the Word of God overflow in my heart and passions? How do I make it more than just the foundation of sermons or devotions? It must become the overflow of my thought life, something that pops up in my mind all day.
—From Joe's journal

About twenty-five years ago, something clicked for me and I realized why I was so intimidated by the concept of meditating all day. I assumed I had to develop this appetite for God's Word on my own. I have ADHD, which makes it hard for me to focus on anything for a long period of time, and I began to realize the only way I would ever be able to meditate on God's Word all day was if my understanding of meditation moved from being about religion and discipline to being about supernaturally-induced appetites and urges.

There was no way I could think about God's Word all day unless some sort of divine intervention took place. Thankfully, God is more than able to help me love His Word.

Let me give you an example of what biblical meditation is like. I love ice cream, and I always have. My favorite flavors are chocolate chip and mint chocolate chip. There's just something about the cool, creamy  texture, that perfect amount of sweetness, and the crunch of the frozen chips.

One Independence Day weekend, we went to visit my mother. There must've been a big sale on Breyers at her local grocery store because she had a freezer full of about twenty containers of six different flavors. After not eating Breyers for almost a full year, I ate four containers in three days. Every time I turned around, I had a bowl full of ice cream. Then, I snuck more of it when no one was looking!

If I had eaten Breyers every time I thought about it, it would've been breakfast, lunch, dinner, and snack. It would've been as natural as breathing. Thinking about this delicious ice cream treat and how I could get more was the kind of fixation the psalmist described when he said he meditated on God's Word all day (v. 97).

I didn't have to force myself to love ice cream. Can you imagine if I had treated loving ice cream the way we tend to treat loving God's Word? "I'm going to become a disciplined lover of ice cream. I don't really love it, but I will force myself to eat it for thirty minutes a day, every day. First thing in the morning, I will get up and eat ice cream. I will think about it, memorize the ingredients, and meditate on it throughout the day because I know it will change my life."

I didn't have to do that. I was born loving ice cream—it's a natural passion of mine. It's the same thing with God's Word. Once you've been given the gift of faith, you will have a hunger for the Word. This gift is a supernatural result of God's Word wedging itself into your life, your heart, and your mind.

An appetite for God's Word is a direct result of God calling you out of darkness and into the light. It's a natural response to the gift of faith, a natural side effect of salvation, redemption, and transformation. This stands in stark contrast to a flawed, pious, religious, even metaphysical definition of meditation.

> *Oh, how I love Your law! It is my* **meditation all the day***. You, through Your commandments, make me wiser than my enemies; for they are ever with me. I have more understanding than all my teachers, for Your testimonies are my meditation. I understand more than the ancients, because I keep Your precepts. I have restrained my feet from every evil way, that I may keep Your word. I have not departed from Your judgments, for You Yourself have taught me. How sweet are Your words to my taste, sweeter than honey to my mouth! Through Your precepts I get understanding; therefore I hate every false way.*
> **—Psalm 119:97–104** (NKJV, emphasis added)

With my ADHD, how do you think I felt when I first started studying all-day meditation in this stanza? It was terrorizing, guilt-inducing, and burdensome. I wondered how in the world I could ever be a good Christian. Anything with the concept of "all day" frightens me—except for eating!

At the time, I felt like I didn't have a chance. I had started thousands of books; I had finished a handful. For decades, I carried this burden of guilt about my inability to meditate all day because I didn't have a biblical understanding of meditation.

I'd been taught that it required quiet, some sort of book, long periods of seclusion, and maybe some kind of instrumental music I couldn't stand. All that can be part of meditation, but those things make up a very tiny percentage of how the psalmist describes biblical meditation in this stanza.

Historical: Hebrew Word Study

Let's dig into the original Hebrew of this stanza so that we can better understand what the psalmist meant by meditating on God's Word all day. The word translated as "meditation" in verse 97 is the Hebrew *siychah,* which means "contemplation or reflection."[45] In the context of this verse, God's law was what the psalmist reflected on all day.

The Hebrew word translated as "all the day," also in verse 97, is *yowm,* which means "while it's hot"—the warm hours of the day.[46] The psalmist desired to focus on God's Word from sunrise to sunset, not just for a few secluded minutes during the day.

Let's think about what it must've been like to spend time in God's Word back in the psalmist's day. It would've been tough to have daily devotions. There was no printing press, no *Our Daily Manna,* no iPhone or Android, no digital Torah to download. Each portion of Scripture had to be hand-copied with perfect accuracy.

Yet the psalmist spent all day with God's Word. It was a dominating influence in his day, and it affected everything he did, thought, and said.

Perhaps when David was king, he had easier access to the Torah than many others did, but he wasn't a scholar or scribe who spent all day copying Scripture. He was a warrior, a ruler, a poet, a musician, and a wretched sinner who committed adultery, murder, and deception. And yet, he managed to inform us of what we need to think about when it comes to meditation.

Biblical meditation starts with asking God to help you focus and prepare your heart and mind before you read His Word. Then you carefully read and keep a receptive mind to what God is telling you. As you go through the day, you wonder and think back on what you read and what it means to your life. Or when something happens, you jump to what the Word of God says about it—not other sources.

So for the psalmist who didn't have the easy access to God's Word, he had to truly focus on those times he did hear or read it. Then he could reflect on and appreciate all God was teaching him.

Theological: The Results of Meditation

Before I give a biblical definition of meditation, let's look at what will happen to your life once you begin meditating on God's Word all day long:

1. You will develop increased wisdom: "You, through Your commandments, make me wiser than my enemies; for they are ever with me. I have more understanding than all my teachers, for Your testimonies are my meditation. I understand more than the ancients, because I keep Your precepts" (Psalm 119:98–100 NKJV).

The Hebrew word translated as "wiser" in verse 98 is *chakam,* which means "to teach wisdom or to make wise."[47] Because the psalmist meditated on God's Word all day, he had more wisdom than he used to have. He also had more wisdom than people who weren't taking the time to meditate on God's Word.

2. You will make better decisions: "I have restrained my feet from every evil way, that I may keep Your word. I have not departed from Your judgments, for You

Yourself have taught me" (Psalm 119:101–102 NKJV).

The word translated as "restrain" in verse 101 is the Hebrew word *kala,* which means "to restrict by act or in word."[48] In other words, you will make better decisions about what you do and what you say.

The Hebrew word translated as "departed" in verse 102 is *cuwr* which means "to turn off, to literally change course at a moment's notice."[49] You can foresee where you are headed and stop, turn around, and go the other direction. One result of meditation is you can change the course of your life at a moment's notice.

3. You will develop righteous passions: "How sweet are Your words to my taste, sweeter than honey to my mouth! Through Your precepts I get understanding; therefore I hate every false way" (Psalm 119:103–104 NKJV).

The word translated as "taste" in verse 103 is the Hebrew *chek,* which refers to the palate or the roof of the mouth.[50] God's Word is not a natural taste but an acquired one, the result of supernatural intervention. Something happens along the way that changes the things you love and desire. As you meditate all day, things that once tasted bitter or unpleasant to you now taste sweet.

The Hebrew word translated as "hate" in verse 104 is *sane,* which means "to hate personally."[51] Notice that while the psalmist said he hated false ways, he did not say he never fell prey to them. We can hate false ways but still struggle with them because we're human.

So clearly we aren't perfect, but we can realize when we do or say things we hate. Before meditation, you don't hate the things your flesh loves, but once you start meditating all day, you begin to despise the things that rob you of joy and life.

There's a contrast, therefore, between the sweet, acquired taste of the Word of God in our mouths and the bitter flavor of those fleshly things we used to love. Wouldn't it be great to have a life filled with increased wisdom, better decisions, and righteous passions? Wouldn't you love to know how to get this life?

What Meditation Looks Like

We get this life by meditating on God's Word all day, but what does that look like? We've already established it doesn't mean reading Scripture non-stop from sunrise to sunset.

1. First, meditation means that God's Word is your desire. You recognize truth is more important than your worldly appetites, as we also see in the book of Job:

> *I have not departed from the commandment of His lips; I have treasured the words of His mouth more than my necessary food.*
>
> —*Job 23:12 (NKJV)*

Job thought about God's Word more often than he thought about eating. This doesn't mean Job read God's Word more than he ate, just that he thought about it. He had an appetite for the truth. Similarly, when we meditate on God's Word all day, we have an appetite, a desire, for the truth. We want to know what the Bible has to say about this or that.

2. Second, meditation means the Word of God is your identity. People know you identify with Jesus and the gospel because of how you respond to truth outwardly. While some people are offended by biblical principles, you love them—even the ones you struggle with.

> *Your words were found, and I ate them, and Your word was to me the joy and rejoicing of my heart; for I am called by Your name, O LORD God of hosts.*
>
> —*Jeremiah 15:16 (NKJV)*

Meditating all day on God's Word makes you look like you follow Jesus. Other people begin to recognize you are a Christian, a Christ-follower.

3. Third, meditation means the Word of God becomes your philosophy. It shapes your worldview. It determines how you process the world around you and how you interact with people, places, and things. It also helps you pinpoint lies:

> *Through Your precepts I get understanding; therefore I hate every false way.*
>
> **—Psalm 119:104** *(NKJV)*

Before meditation on God's Word took its place in your heart as a result of the gift of faith, you were blind to many of these false ways. Now, however, you see them and process information like a child of God.

4. Fourth, meditation means God's Word becomes your dialogue. If you never have anything to say about God's Word, it's because you aren't meditating on it.

> *Moreover He said to me, "Son of man, eat what you find; eat this scroll, and go, speak to the house of Israel." So I opened my mouth, and He caused me to eat that scroll. And He said to me, "Son of man, feed your belly, and fill your stomach with this scroll that I give you." So I ate, and it was in my mouth like honey in sweetness. Then He said to me: "Son of man, go to the house of Israel and speak with My words to them."*
>
> **—Ezekiel 3:1–4** *(NKJV)*

When you meditate on God's Word all day, you start to sound like the Bible when you speak. You talk about biblical concepts. You love to talk about how you were redeemed and the changes God has made in your life. You

like to talk about faith and grace, and you have discussions
with other people about God's Word.

> *The good person out of the good treasure of his heart pro-*
> *duces good, and the evil person out of his evil treasure*
> *produces evil, for out of the abundance of the heart his*
> *mouth speaks.*
>
> **—Luke 6:45**

Devotional: Meditation Is a Gift from God

There are two concepts I'd like to leave you with about
meditating on God's Word all day.

1. First, if you're not meditating on God's Word all
day, you're not growing as you should. It's not just the
fact that you sit down for a few minutes with the Bible—
that's part of meditation, but it's just a tiny fraction of it.

The psalmist meditated on God's Word all day long,
from sunrise to sunset. But wait, don't most people work
during the day? How are we supposed to be reading the
Bible at the same time? What's fascinating is that meditating all day enables you to do your work from a biblical
perspective. It simply means returning to the Word for answers to your questions throughout the day. If you aren't
sure what to do, you remember Proverbs 4:18 says, "But
the path of the just is like the shining sun, that shines ever
brighter unto the perfect day" (NKJV).

That means as you continue on your way things become clearer. That is meditation. You allow God's Word
to instruct and influence you.

The Word of God should be sweet to your taste. If it
isn't, there could be a problem. I don't mean to alarm you,
but I think the truth is this: if there isn't some element of
meditation all day beginning to develop in your life, it's
probably because you haven't been given the gift of faith

that is a direct result of God saving you.

2. Second, meditating all day on God's Word is a direct result of the gifts of faith and spiritual life. For years, I thought meditation was something I had to achieve on my own. I felt like I had to force myself to be a good meditator. Wasn't that arrogant?

Meditation is not something you achieve, something to brag about. It's a natural reaction to the gift of faith. It's not a sign of your spiritual maturity—it's a sign of your miraculous transformation. If there's an opportunity to meditate all day, it's not because you are good but because God is good.

The psalmist didn't have this relationship with God's Word because he was some sort of spiritual giant. In fact, he was a terrible sinner. But he had this relationship with God's Word because of what God had done in his life, despite who he was. The same is true of us.

Through the gift of faith, you will become someone who meditates all day. God's Word will be in your thoughts, your words, your actions, your decisions, and your passions. It will become your desire, your identity, your philosophy, and your dialogue. It will encompass every aspect of your life.

I hope this begins to relieve a burden about what meditation means. It's not a matter of Eastern mysticism; it's God's Word supernaturally wedging itself into your heart, mind, and life. Everywhere you turn, you hear it and see it.

WORKBOOK

Chapter Thirteen Questions

Question: What images or ideas come to mind when you hear the word *meditation*? What are some misconceptions that you have had about meditation, including scriptural meditation? What are some things, good or bad, that you naturally meditate on without trying? What can this show you about the nature of true biblical meditation?

_____

_____

_____

_____

_____

_____

_____

_____

Question: What are some ways God's Word is changing your thoughts, speech, and actions? Do others identify you as a person whose life is built on the Bible?

_____

_____

_____

_____

_____

_____

_____

_____

_____

_____

Question: What are some reasons someone might not have a supernatural love and desire for Scripture? If this is true in a person's life, what are some prayers and decisions that person could make to see transformation in their relationship with God's Word?

_____

_____

_____

_____

_____

_____

_____

_____

_____

_____

_____

_____

Action: While meditation is a supernatural result of the gift of faith and God's work in your life, memorizing Scripture allows the Holy Spirit to easily bring it to your mind when it is needed. Choose a Scripture memory plan to use or a passage to begin memorizing.

_____

_____

_____

_____

_____

_____

_____

_____

_____

_____

Chapter Thirteen Notes

CHAPTER FOURTEEN

Nun—Walking in the Light

Your word is a lamp to my feet and a light to my path. I have sworn and confirmed that I will keep Your righteous judgments. I am afflicted very much; revive me, O LORD, according to Your word. Accept, I pray, the freewill offerings of my mouth, O LORD, and teach me Your judgments. My life is continually in my hand, yet I do not forget Your law. The wicked have laid a snare for me, yet I have not strayed from Your precepts. Your testimonies I have taken as a heritage forever, for they are the rejoicing of my heart. I have inclined my heart to perform Your statutes forever, to the very end.

—Psalm 119:105–112 *(NKJV)*

Looking at this fourteenth stanza, titled "Nun," I was overwhelmed by the concept of light in the Word of God and its connection to Jesus and how beautifully these two concepts are illustrated in this stanza.

The world is a place of darkness. Often, it's so dark we don't know what to do, where to go, or who or what to turn to. Christ, however, is the light of life, our guide through the dark places.

To illustrate this concept and what it means especially to a new believer, I'd like to share a piece titled "The Paths of Life" written by my dear friend Chad, who is married to my niece Stephanie. Chad was the first young person I had the privilege of leading to Christ when we first moved back to Florida in 1999.

God saved Chad in the spring of his freshman year of high school, and he wrote this piece in the fall of his sophomore year:

> Picture a long, straight path that's well lit, smooth ground. It's a comfortable place, a safe place to travel. But on the sides of this path are stones, rocks, and other dark paths that lead nowhere. You see, I was born on the dark paths, the dead-end paths. In fact, we are all born there. All my life, I had this desire to stay on the dark paths. I had heard about this well-lit path, but I never cared anything about it. I liked the darkness and the things in the darkness. They felt good. They were fun, even though they always caused me pain sooner or later.
>
> One day, Jesus began calling me to His path, and He showed me what it was like to walk on it. His path felt safe and peaceful. I thought to myself, "Maybe I should stay here." While I was walking this path, I heard a familiar voice calling me from the darkness. I was very willing to return to that darkness. It felt nice and smooth against my skin, and it was just cool enough to feel refreshing. I always enjoyed the initial feeling the darkness gave me. I loved the dark coolness and the smoothness. It made me forget about the light of Jesus' path for a while.
>
> But one day, the pleasure of the darkness turned to severe pain. It scared me, and I ran back toward the light of Jesus' path. He calmed me, soothed my pain, and began to teach me. He warned me about the darkness, how it led nowhere but death and always let you down, causing much pain along the way. He taught me how the light would never let me down and would lead me to joy and redemption.
>
> But for some reason, those dark paths kept calling me.

And by my very nature, I would wander back into darkness, back to the place I was born, getting hurt repeatedly. I was stuck in a pattern: I would get hurt, I'd run to the light and get temporary relief from the pain, and then I would leave when the voices from the dead-end path would call me back.

One day, while I was enjoying the darkness and the cool, smooth pleasure of it on my skin, it seemed more enjoyable than ever before. I was so confused. How could something that was so good be so bad, so dangerous, as Jesus had tried to tell me? My whole life was centered on enjoying this feeling in the dark. How could it be wrong? I was ready to wrap my arms around the darkness and embrace it, to fully commit to it.

Suddenly, I heard a loud voice warning me. I was startled at first and, frankly, a bit annoyed. There was Jesus, facing me and shining a huge light into the darkness. At first, I was blinded when I looked into His light. Jesus instructed me, "Don't look here; turn and look at what you were ready to embrace, what has been so tempting all your life."

Honestly, I was afraid to look, but when I did, I could not believe what I saw. I saw a terrible serpent with massive fangs and wicked, sinister eyes that were full of wrath and hatred for me. I couldn't believe I'd been so blind, how the darkness had hidden the true danger from me. What I thought was bringing me pleasure and comfort had been luring me into a trap that would've cost me my very soul. Talk about feeling betrayed! But I still couldn't just leave it. It was who I was, where I was born. It was my very identity, this darkness.

So, what did Jesus do? He began calling to me with a strong, irresistible voice. Just in the nick of time, I felt His hand grab hold of mine. He yanked me out of the darkness. It was at that point I realized I had become a child of God, a child of the light with full vision of what the world was around me. This was my new identity, my new path, my new way of life.

To this day, we walk together, His light showing me each road, each step to take. Sometimes I think about wandering, thinking I can handle myself in the darkness now because I can see the snakes. But when I do, He's holding onto my hand, never letting me get too far down the paths of darkness. When I stumble, He catches me and sets me back on my feet in the light of life.

The enemy always makes darkness seem appealing and desirable. He creates the illusion that things in this dark world are the light we seek. However, Jesus is the true light and will stop at nothing to free His chosen ones from our blindness. Therefore, it is critical that we understand more about what this *light* is.

Historical: Hebrew Word Study

*Your word is a **lamp** to my **feet** and a **light** to my **path**. I have sworn and confirmed that I will keep Your righteous judgments. I am afflicted very much; revive me, O LORD, according to Your word. Accept, I pray, the freewill offerings of my mouth, O LORD, and teach me Your judgments. My life is continually in my hand, yet I do not forget Your law. The wicked have laid a snare for me, yet I have not strayed from Your precepts. Your testimonies I have taken as a heritage forever, for they are the rejoicing of my heart. I have inclined my heart to perform Your statutes forever, to the very end.*

—Psalm 119:105–112 (NKJV, emphasis added)

In this stanza, the psalmist provides two different images of light. By digging into the original Hebrew, we can better understand what the psalmist is communicating here.

The word translated as "lamp" in verse 105 is the Hebrew *ner*, which refers to a small light like a lamp or a candle.[52] That's the first concept of light presented in this stanza, as the psalmist describes God's Word as a lamp to his feet.

In that same verse, the Hebrew word translated as "feet" is *regel,* which means foot—as in, the sort of foot that you walk with.[53] The implication here is of a person walking slowly, carefully, in the darkness, step by step.

For the psalmist, the Word of God was a dimmer, smaller lamp to his darkened path, lighting his way step by step. He couldn't see what was further ahead, but he knew where he was putting his foot at the moment was safe and secure.

This is the first image of light: a lamp or candle in the darkness that enables the psalmist to live cautiously in stressful circumstances, one moment at a time.

The Hebrew word translated as "light" in verse 105 is *owr,* which means "bright, clear day, the morning sun."[54] The word translated as "path" in this same verse is *nathiyb,* meaning "a path, a well-beaten track, a road of travel, or a highway."[55]

This is the second image of light: the sun or the clear light of day that illuminated the psalmist's path as he walked easily down a well-known road of travel.

The Word of God lit the psalmist's life in different ways in two different circumstances. It was a lesser light at night and a brighter light during the day. God's Word showed him the direction he should travel on the road of life, helping him to see the bigger picture, but it also guided him step by step in the dark paths of uncertainty. No matter what the psalmist's circumstances were, whether it was dark or broad daylight, he walked in the light of God's Word.

Theological: Jesus, the Light of the World

Did you know there were two types of light at creation?

> *Then God made two great lights: the greater light to rule the day, and the lesser light to rule the night. He made the stars also. God set them in the firmament of the heavens to give light on the earth, and to rule over the day and over the night, and to divide the light from the darkness. And God saw that it was good.*
>
> **—Genesis 1:16–18** *(NKJV)*

There is no question in my mind that the psalmist was thinking of creation when he wrote this stanza. He was not only talking about the light of God's Word but also about the light of creation at the same time. Talk about poetic genius!

The psalmist was essentially saying the Word of God was like a moon at night and a sun during the day. What an incredible song about light in this album we call Psalm 119. If this was released by a record company today, this stanza would be one of the album's first singles.

1. Jesus is the creator of that light. In Scripture, we see this idea of a heavenly light, this moon and sun, that is transferred into the hearts and minds of those He has called out of the darkness. Recall John 1:3–5:

> *All things were made through him, and without him was not any thing made that was made. In him was life, and the life was the light of men. The light shines in the darkness, and the darkness has not overcome it.*

Do you see what the psalmist has done here? Jesus created this light—both lights. It says in other places in the Bible, such as Colossians 1:16 and John 1:1, that Jesus is God and Creator. The psalmist was therefore singing about the Savior as well as creation.

2. Jesus is also the source of light. God's Word brackets the creation of the sun and the moon with the source of true light at the end of time.

And the city has no need of sun or moon to shine on it, for the glory of God gives it light, and its lamp is the Lamb. By its light will the nations walk, and the kings of the earth will bring their glory into it, and its gates will never be shut by day—and there will be no night there.
—Revelation 21:23–25

Isn't that an amazing picture? I've long been familiar with the words of Psalm 119:105, but it wasn't until recently I realized the psalmist wasn't only talking about God's Word being a light, but that he was also making a connection to creation, to the sun and moon.

I love the way the Word of God brackets this. At the beginning, there were two lights, the moon and the sun. *At the end, they are no longer needed. There is only one light: Jesus, the light of the world.*

The Benefits of Good Lighting

Again Jesus spoke to them, saying, "I am the light of the world. Whoever follows me will not walk in darkness, but will have the light of life."
—John 8:12

We need to understand a few things about spiritual light. Make no mistake—when God's Word first shines into your life, it hurts your eyes, like when you walk out of a dark movie theater and must adjust to the daylight.

When God first shines the light of salvation into your life, it's kind of annoying. You want to stay in the darkness because it seems like such a great place, but the light shows you where you're headed, that remaining in the darkness will only lead to danger, death, and destruction.

The second step into the light, however, is when you start to see clearly. The initial exposure to the light of

God's Word is very uncomfortable, but as our spiritual eyes—the ones we've been enlightened with by the Word of God and the Holy Spirit—adjust to the brightness, it transforms our lives in several ways.

1. The light of God's Word gives us hope during times of affliction: "I am afflicted very much; revive me, O LORD, according to Your word" (Psalm 119:107 NKJV).

Life and light are synonymous in this stanza. Many people become lost and aimless and feel alone in dark times.

That's life in spiritual darkness. It's defeating, draining, confusing, and painful. It's hopeless without the light of life, the light of Jesus, the light of the Word. Light, the Word, Jesus, life—they're all the same. When the light of God's Word is your guide during dark times, it gives you hope.

You know there is literally a light at the end of the tunnel, and that gives you hope for revival, restoration, and redemption. Even though it's pitch-black, there is one light shining there, and that's enough to encourage you to take the next step.

2. The light of God's Word enables us to live in gratitude: "Accept, I pray, the freewill offerings of my mouth, O LORD, and teach me Your judgments" (Psalm 119:108 NKJV).

The light allows you to recognize where your blessings come from, and it's not from the dark pleasures of the world that were destroying you.

Your vision is now clear, and you know why. Because of the light that has made it clear where your blessings come from, you are inspired to direct thankfulness and praise to the One who deserves it. That's what a freewill offering is. It's not something you do out of guilt, religious compliance, or because you're trying to make up for wrongdoings. It's joyfully showing your gratitude to God who has blessed you.

A freewill offering is not an offering of repentance, and it's not made to elicit God's favor in some way. It's simply the result of light that has given you love for the Father of lights.

> *Every good gift and every perfect gift is from above, coming down from the Father of lights, with whom there is no variation or shadow due to change.*
> **—James 1:17**

> *Through him then let us continually offer up a sacrifice of praise to God, that is, the fruit of lips that acknowledge his name.*
> **—Hebrews 13:15**

3. The light of God's Word gives us wisdom during the night: "My life is continually in my hand, yet I do not forget Your law. The wicked have laid a snare for me, yet I have not strayed from Your precepts" (Psalm 119:109–110 NKJV).

In this context, "stray" means to take a step that is off the lit path.

The enemy has laid snares and traps for us. These could be immoral relationships, addictions, the love of money, pride, arrogance, or any number of things. But because of the light of God's Word, we can walk step by step without straying into a path of darkness.

The enemy has this uncanny ability to deceive us, sneak up on us, and burn our lives to the ground. He thrives in darkness like a fish thrives in water. He breathes it through his evil gills, and he loves it when we step into his domain.

He's ready to lay traps for you, but the Word of God gives you wisdom during the night. The light of God's

Word points out the traps. "Don't step there! There's arrogance. There's love of money. There's addiction or immorality." The light of God's Word on the dark path gives you wisdom during the night to see the traps set for you, all along the way.

> I will bring the blind by a way they did not know; I will lead them in paths they have not known. I will make darkness light before them, and crooked places straight. These things I will do for them, and not forsake them.
> **—Isaiah 42:16** *(NKJV)*

This is the role of the light of God's Word in our lives, giving us guidance step by step and wisdom during the night.

> Jesus answered, "Are there not twelve hours in the day? If anyone walks in the day, he does not stumble, because he sees the light of this world. But if anyone walks in the night, he stumbles, because the light is not in him."
> **—John 11:9–10**

4. The light of God's Word gives us stability: "Your testimonies I have taken as a heritage forever, for they are the rejoicing of my heart. I have inclined my heart to perform Your statutes forever, to the very end" (Psalm 119:111–112 NKJV).

This means we hold on to God's Word until we are done with our journey.

> If we say we have fellowship with him while we walk in darkness, we lie and do not practice the truth. But if we walk in the light, as he is in the light, we have fellowship with one another, and the blood of Jesus his Son cleanses

us from all sin.

—1 John 1:6–7

Living in the light of God's Word doesn't mean bad things won't happen. It means when bad things happen, there is a measure of stability. You're no longer being battered to and fro, trying to keep your balance. No matter what takes place, you can face it with stability, wisdom, and discernment. In other words, you're not a drama king or queen.

Jesus is the living Word of God. He's also the source of light the psalmist sings about. It's the gift of faith, the calling of God, that brings the light to our path and into our highway of living.

> *So Jesus said to them, "The light is among you for a little while longer. Walk while you have the light, lest darkness overtake you. The one who walks in the darkness does not know where he is going. While you have the light, believe in the light, that you may become sons of light."*
> *—John 12:35–36*

Once we are called by God into His light, we receive all the inestimable benefits of good spiritual lighting.

> *But you are a chosen race, a royal priesthood, a holy nation, a people for his own possession, that you may proclaim the excellencies of him who called you out of darkness into his marvelous light.*
> *—1 Peter 2:9*

Devotional: Taking the First Steps

Once, you were walking in darkness. You were living life on the path of darkness, a path filled with traps and snares. You had no interest in light, but then suddenly, the light of God's Word through the power of the Holy Spirit, Jesus Christ, comes down and warns you to look at where you're going.

Your first reaction is to tell Him to get that light out of your eyes, but then you look at where you were heading, and you realize you don't want to go there. You start to adjust your steps and follow His light.

Jesus leads you onto the path of life, which is a highway, and your eyes continue to adjust to the light as you step into the brightness of day. As you continue to walk in the light, you enjoy life more abundantly.

WORKBOOK

Chapter Fourteen Questions

Question: How have you experienced Christ as the light in the darkness of this world? When have you tried to hide in the familiar, comfortable darkness, and what brought you to the light? What gave you the courage to deal with all that it exposed?

_____

_____

_____

_____

_____

_____

_____

_____

_____

_____

Question: Describe a time when the light of God's Word gave you hope in a dark situation. What are some ways the light of God's Word has inspired you to praise God?

_____

_____

_____

_____

_____

_____

_____

_____

_____

_____

Question: People stumble and fall easily in the darkness. Proper lighting gives stability. How does the light of the Word stabilize your thoughts and emotions? How does it bring stability to your relationships and responsibilities?

_____

_____

_____

_____

_____

_____

_____

_____

_____

_____

_____

_____

Action: Take a look around you at all the different sources of light we use in our modern world. What can each of these tell you about the role of God's Word in your life?

_____

_____

_____

_____

_____

_____

_____

_____

_____

Chapter Fourteen Notes

CHAPTER FIFTEEN

Samekh—Shields Up

When I was a kid, I loved the original *Star Trek* series. I would watch it as if it was happening in real time. The shields have always been my favorite part of that series, and I'd get mad when the captain wouldn't put his  shields up in time. "What are you doing? Put the shields up! It's Klingons!"

I love that no matter where they were in the universe, they had this special device to put up for protection. At the time, I didn't understand the true significance of us also having a spiritual shield.

*I hate the **double-minded**, but I love Your law. You are my **hiding place** and my **shield**; I hope in Your word. Depart from me, you evildoers, for I will keep the commandments of my God! Uphold me according to Your word, that I may live; and do not let me be ashamed of my hope. Hold me up, and I shall be safe, and I shall observe Your statutes continually. You reject all those who stray from Your statutes, for their deceit is falsehood. You put away all the wicked of* *the earth like dross; therefore I love Your testimonies. My flesh trembles for fear of You, and I am afraid of Your judgments.*

—Psalm 119:113–120 *(NKJV, emphasis added)*

There are dark times in our lives, and we can't avoid them. They are part of living in a fallen world that is waiting for redemption. Whether you realize it or not, you need a shield from the world, a place to go and hide.

I need to constantly evaluate what things I hate. If I begin to show signs of tolerance of sin, selfishness, etc., I am allowing my love for the Word of God to be compromised.

—From Joe's journal

In this fifteenth stanza, titled "Samekh," the psalmist teaches that the only way to navigate this world system is by having a shelter and a shield. That shield is knowing the promises of hope and redemption in God's Word and living a life of obedience to its precepts.

Historical: Hebrew Word Study

David was an expert on shields. In the ESV translation of the Bible, the word "shield" is used seventy-four times in the Old Testament and once in the New Testament. The words "hiding place" or "shelter" are used a combined eighteen times in the Old Testament.

David was very familiar with times of sadness and fear. In the course of his life, he dealt with an angry Saul, the Philistines, his son Absalom who tried to take the kingdom from him, and even his own wickedness. He knew how desperately he needed to connect to God's Word to keep his mind sane when terrible things came upon him.

Let's look at some original Hebrew in this stanza. The word translated as "double-minded" in verse 113 is the Hebrew *çeeph,* which means "divided in mind or skeptical."[56] The psalmist is referring to people who are paralyzed by doubt, a terrorized state that distorts their will and leads them into despair and worry.

Without God's Word, the world makes us double-minded and unstable. Without a shield, the world makes us grope in fear, anger, resentment, bitterness, and judgment of others. The psalmist hated what those things did to distract him from God's Word. He recognized that without God's Word, the world would make him an unstable mess.

The psalmist gives two ways that the Word of God protects him from the instability that the world creates in his life. The word translated as "hiding place" in verse 114 is the Hebrew *cether,* which refers to a place to hide carefully.[57] It conveys the idea of a dwelling place, a house where we can escape from the world's attacks, rest, and catch our breath.

The word translated as "shield," also in verse 114, is the Hebrew *magen,* which refers to a shield or armor, like the scaly hide of a crocodile.[58] It conveys the idea of the Word of God protecting you during a fight.

God's Word protected the psalmist both as a shelter and as a shield, keeping him from being distracted or wounded by the world.

Theological: The Protection of God's Word

The Word of God is a shelter and a shield from many things.

1. First, it is a shelter and a shield from evil: "Depart from me, you evildoers, for I will keep the commandments of my God" (Psalm 119:115 NKJV).

When God's Word is your shield, it gives you the ability to see evildoers coming and the courage to separate from people who would lead you astray from God. You realize evil is in this world and understand what the consequences could be if you associate with it, and so you turn away from it.

2. *Second, the Word of God is a shelter and a shield from shame:* "Uphold me according to Your word, that I may live; and do not let me be ashamed of my hope (Psalm 119:116 NKJV).

God's Word gives you an eye for eternity. It enables you to have courage and hope to live as though eternity has already arrived.

Even in times of failure, God's Word will shield you from shame because your hope of eternal redemption can be recognized and realized now. It's not just something you're waiting for—it's something you are confident will happen. Therefore, you are sheltered and shielded from the pain that comes from losing hope.

3. *Third, the Word of God is a shelter and shield from consequences:* "Hold me up, and I shall be safe, and I shall observe Your statutes continually" (Psalm 119:117 NKJV).

God's Word preserves and protects you from many arrows and slings of this world that would otherwise put you in danger, cause you pain, bring consequences upon your life, or make you unstable, double-minded, and gripped with fear, resentment, bitterness, and shame.

4. *Fourth, the Word of God is a shelter and a shield from judgment:* "You reject all those who stray from Your statutes, for their deceit is falsehood. You put away all the wicked of the earth like dross; therefore I love Your testimonies. My flesh trembles for fear of You, and I am afraid of Your judgments" (Psalm 119:118–120 NKJV).

I don't really talk about judgment much—not because I don't believe it's real but because it's kind of scary. However, God's Word not only shields and protects us during life's storms, but also in times of judgment. What's the point of forgiveness and redemption if they don't protect you from judgment?

El Capitan in Yosemite National Park is a one-mile-high cliff with a sheer drop. It attracts mountaineers from all over the world, especially in the autumn. In September 2017, a granite slab the size of an apartment building—about a hundred feet by a  hundred feet—separated from the cliff face and fell to the ground, killing one person and injuring another.[59]

In Revelation 6:16, those facing the sixth seal judgment of God cry out for the mountains and rocks to fall on them to hide them from God's wrath. They would rather be crushed and killed than face God as judge.

When you trust God's promises to you, you are sheltered and shielded from His righteous judgments. You don't have to be fearful of what judgment could do to you because you understand you have been saved from judgment by the gift of faith and redemption. The message of God's grace in His Word shields and hides us through the work of His Son on the cross.

Enlightened fear of God's judgment motivates us to remain shielded and sheltered by the concepts in His Word.

Therefore, my beloved, as you have always obeyed, so now, not only as in my presence but much more in my absence, work out your own salvation with fear and trembling.
—Philippians 2:12

This does not mean you earn your salvation. Rather, because you have taken the time to understand your salvation and what it means, you will understand God's judgment and how you have been granted escape from it.

I think about that image in Revelation of people wanting the rocks to crush and hide them from the wrath of God's judgment, and I am so thankful that, through the gift of faith and the gospel, God's Word shelters and shields me from that. Imagine what it would be like to meet God and for Him to be your judge, not your Father. That's scary stuff.

Using Your Shield

The only shield or shelter that will work is our relationship with God's Word. Unfortunately, many Christians turn to other things they think will preserve and protect them: relationships, money, or their careers.

That's the spiritual equivalent of a child pulling the sheets over their head because they think it will protect them from monsters. It does nothing. The only solid, failproof hiding place is the truth of God's Word, which will protect us from evil, shame, consequences, and judgment.

So how do we use our shield? Proverbs 30:5 (NKJV) tells us, "Every word of God is pure; He is a shield to those who put their trust in Him." To get the most out of your shield, you need to be familiar with it. It doesn't do any good to go into battle with a shield you don't even know how to hold properly. It's pointless.

You need to have an extensive, systematic, disciplined approach to being exposed to God's Word so that you know how your shield works. That can be studying independently, being discipled by another person, listening to sermons or music based on Scripture, or any other method that works for you. Constant exposure to the shelter and the shield begins the process of allowing every word to be proven true.

This goes back to one of our earlier lessons in Psalm

119: "Establish Your word to Your servant, who is devoted to fearing You" (v. 38 NKJV). If you are not consistently exposing yourself to God's Word, you are not sheltered or shielded.

Paul writes that we should pick up our shields in "all circumstances" so that we "can extinguish all the flaming darts of the evil one" (Ephesians 6:16). The enemy wants to lure us out from our shelter, out from behind our shield, which is obedience and love for God's Word. As the psalmist says, if we stay behind the Word of God and are obedient to it, it will make us wiser than our enemies (Psalm 119:98).

When a believer is failing, or has failed, it is likely they are not in the shelter of obedience to the Word of God. Having God's Word as your shield, however, doesn't mean you won't experience difficult times. There will be flaming darts from the evil one. Since we don't always know when a flaming dart is headed our way, it's best to keep our shield up all the time.

What are the results of using your shield? Unlike TV and movies, the powerful weapons of the world cannot be used successfully against your shield and your shelter.

"No weapon formed against you shall prosper, and every tongue which rises against you in judgment you shall condemn. This is the heritage of the servants of the LORD, and their righteousness is from Me," says the LORD.
—Isaiah 54:17 (NKJV)

I love how the Word of God promises that there is nothing the enemy can do to destroy your hope if you use it as a shelter when you are resting and a shield when you are fighting. Your hope will not be put to shame, and you'll be able to escape evil, shame, consequences, and judgment.

I love, too, what David says about his shield:

> *The LORD is my strength and my shield; my heart trusted in Him, and I am helped; therefore my heart greatly rejoices, and with my song I will praise Him. The LORD is their strength, and He is the saving refuge of His anointed.*
> —**Psalm 28:7–8** *(NKJV)*

The Hebrew word David used for *shield* in this passage is the same word used for *shield* in Psalm 119.

Devotional: Don't Drop Your Guard

We always need to keep our shields up because the temptations of the world are all around us. Don't take them down, don't come out from behind them. Don't allow yourself to be lulled into a false sense of security, thinking you've spent enough time exposed to God's Word and you can take a break.

You can change how you're exposing yourself to God's Word, but don't ever take a break. Maybe one week you've done a lot of studying, so the next week you listen to music with lyrics from Scripture. Whatever it is, you need to be exposed to the concepts in God's Word.

How do we make sure our shields are up? We do this by eating all day, by feeding on the Word of God. I did an experiment with a small group of people to help them redefine meditation—in other words, how to keep their shields up. I asked them to take a day and fill out a short survey of how many times they read God's Word, thought about God's Word, thought about God, or thought about a principle in God's Word.

Three people responded that by noon they had done one or more of these things more than thirty times! That was both awesome and supernatural. People without the gift of faith don't do that.

Now, this isn't a call to be legalistic. There's no set number of times in a day that we're obligated to focus intentionally on God's Word. The point is, the ability to keep our shields up is a direct result of the gift of faith.

Jesus has equipped us with all we need to withstand the enemy's attacks, but we can't wait until an attack is already upon us—we must keep our shield ready. It's crucial we understand how our shields work and how to use them.

The better we understand what a powerful weapon we have in God's Word, the better prepared we are to engage our shields, rebuff our enemy, and preserve our hope in Christ.

Chapter Fifteen Questions

Question: What are some examples of how you have faced double-mindedness or a conflicted heart because of the worries of this world? How are you unstable without God's Word?

_____

_____

_____

_____

_____

_____

_____

_____

_____

_____

_____

Question: God's Word is a shelter and shield from evil, shame, consequences, and judgment. What are specific biblical promises that speak to each of these dangers and God's strength to help you overcome them?

_____

_____

_____

_____

_____

_____

_____

_____

_____

_____

Question: Evaluate your exposure to God's Word. In what ways are you building it into every day? What are some additional, practical ways that you can hear, receive, study, learn, memorize, and meditate on God's Word?

_____

_____

_____

_____

_____

_____

_____

_____

_____

_____

_____

Action: Draw or find a picture of a shield or a refuge (shelter) and put it on a blank notecard. Write Psalm 119:114 next to the picture. Send the notecard to someone who is going through a difficult time, with a personal note inside sharing how God's Word has helped you during times of instability and uncertainty and encouraging your friend not to drop their shield.

_____

_____

_____

_____

_____

_____

_____

_____

_____

Chapter Fifteen Notes

CHAPTER SIXTEEN

Ayin—The Cosigner

When you cosign for someone, you agree to pay a debt they have taken on in the event they're unable to repay it. How do you feel about cosigning for someone? What would it take for you to be comfortable cosigning on someone's loan? Would it need to be a family member or at least a close friend? Would you cosign for a stranger or for someone you'd only met a few times?

What about asking someone to cosign for you? Have you ever had someone cosign for you? How did it make you feel when someone signed for you, essentially saying, "If this person can't make good, I got 'em"? Were you able to make good on it, or did you fail to meet the obligations?

In my life, there's only been one person who was willing to cosign on a debt for me: my grandfather. I was eighteen years and seven months old, and he agreed to be surety for me, to cosign for my first car loan so that I could buy a brand-new 1986

Shelby Charger. I got so many tickets in that car!

I love telling people about my granddad and how he cosigned that loan for me because it was one of the most meaningful things he ever did for me before he died when I was about 20. I had a special re-  lationship with him, and I understood what it meant for him to cosign and why he did it.

But as much as I loved him and was motivated to honor him, in the end I defaulted on that loan. The car got wrecked, and there was no way I could pay the bill. But here was the problem: my granddad had died before this happened, so I had to bear the full burden of that responsibility. It took me years to overcome it.

Had my grandfather been alive, he would've paid my debt, but he was just a man and died. That's the difference between my granddad and Jesus. Jesus died and was resurrected. He conquered death and paid our debt in full. He is the ultimate cosigner.

If Jesus has cosigned for your debt of sin, if He has given you surety for righteousness, then the enemy can do nothing to void that contract, as much as he wants to. Our cosigner lives, and He will never die. He will always be there to pay the debt we owe.

I was highly motivated to honor my grandfather. I never thought I would default on that loan because I loved that man. But I'm human. Things happen. I lost jobs, I drove too fast in the rain, and I was not able to pay my debt.

That's us when we try to please God through religion. You can be as motivated as you like, but you will not succeed. Instead, you need to recognize your righteousness is the righteousness of Christ He put in your name because

He cosigned for you. He was a pledge for good. He was surety. Thank God we have the ultimate cosigner.

In this sixteenth stanza, titled "Ayin," the psalmist is talking about someone signing for him. Every time I read this stanza, I remember my grandfather.

> *I have done justice and righteousness; do not leave me to my oppressors. Be surety for Your servant for good; do not let the proud oppress me. My eyes fail from seeking Your salvation and Your righteous word. Deal with Your servant according to Your mercy, and teach me Your statutes. I am Your servant; give me understanding, that I may know Your testimonies. It is time for You to act, O LORD, for they have regarded Your law as void. Therefore I love Your commandments more than gold, yes, than fine gold! Therefore all Your precepts concerning all things I consider to be right; I hate every false way.*
> —**Psalm 119:121–128** *(NKJV, emphasis added)*

Historical: Hebrew Word Study

The psalmist had incredible confidence in his standing before God. Let's look at some of the original Hebrew in this stanza to better understand why the psalmist was so confident.

The word translated "justice" in verse 121 is the Hebrew *mishpat*, which refers to a judiciary verdict.[60] In this context, the psalmist says he has done what was just according to the law of Moses.

Also in verse 121, the Hebrew word translated as "righteousness" is *tsedeq*, meaning "that which is right morally."[61] The psalmist considered himself to be right not just legally but also morally.

Lastly, the word translated as "surety" in verse 122 is the Hebrew *arab*, meaning "to cosign or be surety, to undertake financial responsibility."[62] Because the psalmist considered himself just according to the law and righteous according to morality, he asked God to be surety for him for good and for righteousness.

The psalmist demonstrated amazing, ridiculous confidence in his standing morally and legally, declaring his life was characterized by just and righteous actions. How could David feel this way? He knew he was a liar, an adulterer, and a murderer, yet, somehow, he has the confidence to say he is just and right. And in that confidence, he asks God to cosign for his own personal righteousness.

David knew his just and righteous standing—his confidence—was tied to God, not to himself. He asked God to be his cosigner for righteousness, so that when he was finally judged for all he had done and was unable to pay the debt for his sin, God, his cosigner, would take responsibility for his debt and pay it. Imagine the relationship, the understanding he must have had with the Father to ask for such a thing!

David understood his connection to God was not based on religion or personal, moral accomplishment. He also knew he could never meet his obligations on that front. He knew he could never perform well enough, but his ridiculous confidence came from the humility of recognizing by faith, which is a gift, his just and righteous standing was a direct result of God being surety for him—cosigning for him.

As a matter of fact, David understood his position of righteousness and justice even during one of his greatest moral failures. When the prophet Nathan confronted him about Bathsheba—the woman with whom he had committed adultery—and Uriah—her husband whom David had killed (2 Samuel 12)—David knew he was ultimately still in a position of righteousness and justice because God had cosigned for him.

This did not mean, however, David was off the hook

for what he had done. He still needed to acknowledge his sins before God and repent of them. Psalm 51, which David wrote during this time, focuses on the need for repentance, declaring God as the only one who can pay the debt of sin.

> *For You do not desire sacrifice, or else I would give it; You do not delight in burnt offering. The sacrifices of God are a broken spirit, a broken and a contrite heart—these, O God, You will not despise.*
>
> **—Psalm 51:16–17** *(NKJV)*

David knew he was not connected to God because of his religion; he was connected to God because he knew he could never be good enough on his own.

Theological: Jesus, Our Cosigner

As Christians, Jesus is our cosigner. Let me give you a legal and moral explanation for why and how our salvation works. It's not simply that Jesus died and resurrected, so we're saved. There's an actual reason He had to die.

Scripture says that being a pledge for good, a cosigner for someone, is a serious commitment that often brings pain.

> *He who is surety for a stranger will suffer, but one who hates being surety is secure.*
>
> **—Proverbs 11:15** *(NKJV)*

Some pastors teach this means you should never cosign for anyone, but that's not what Scripture is teaching here. It's simply saying that when you do cosign for someone, you will suffer pain and loss. If you don't cosign for someone, you will be secure.

Jesus could have been secure, but He put up the security He could've had so our relationship with God could be restored. He was willing to suffer pain. He agreed to be our pledge for good, to pay the price we would not be able to pay, and He suffered on the cross.

Paul describes this concept in many places in his letters.

> For the wages of sin is death, but the free gift of God is eternal life in Christ Jesus our Lord.
>
> —*Romans 6:23*

You have a bill to pay if you want redemption and eternal life, and to pay that bill, you have to die. But the problem is that when you're dead, you're dead. Jesus, through His death in our place, gives us life.

> For our sake he made him to be sin who knew no sin, so that in him we might become the righteousness of God.
>
> —*2 Corinthians 5:21*

This is like Psalm 119:121, where David talked about how he had done what was just and right. He knew his righteousness was not his own, but he was able to say those things because God was his pledge of good, his cosigner, his surety.

David said his righteousness was that of the God of the universe. Isn't that wild? Talk about confidence! Because God was his cosigner, he was able declare he was as righteous as God despite being a murderer, among many other things

Over and over, Paul addresses this concept of someone cosigning for us:

Indeed, I count everything as loss because of the surpassing worth of knowing Christ Jesus my Lord. For his sake I have suffered the loss of all things and count them as rubbish, in order that I may gain Christ and be found in him, not having a righteousness of my own that comes from the law, but that which comes through faith in Christ, the righteousness from God that depends on faith.

—Philippians 3:8–9

How should we respond when someone cosigns for us? The appropriate response is to live in gratitude. There's a great example of this in the story of Onesimus.

In Philemon, which is just one chapter long, Paul wrote to a wealthy man named Philemon who had a slave named Onesimus. Onesimus had stolen money from Philemon and run away. By God's sovereign plan, Onesimus encountered Paul, who led him to Christ, discipled him for a time, and then told him he needed to return to Philemon and make things right. To help facilitate Onesimus's return, Paul offered to repay anything he might owe Philemon:

So if you consider me your partner, receive him as you would receive me. If he has wronged you at all, or owes you anything, charge that to my account. I, Paul, write this with my own hand: I will repay it—to say nothing of your owing me even your own self. Yes, brother, I want some benefit from you in the Lord. Refresh my heart in Christ.

—Philemon 1:17–20

Can you imagine what Onesimus must have been feeling? Paul wrote him a letter to give to Philemon that would explain the situation and made it clear Paul would repay any debt he owed, clearing the way for the two men to be reconciled.

Paul knew the reconciliation between Onesimus and

Philemon would cost him money, and he was willing to pay it. What a great picture of the love Jesus has for us!

I remember going down to the dealership with my credit application, thinking there was no way they'd give me a car loan. My mom told me to just go ahead and submit it, and it came back approved. I asked her how that had happened, if she had cosigned my loan. She said, "No, your granddad did." I was overwhelmed with love for him—not because I was getting a new car but because I knew he'd stuck his neck out for me.

It was so humbling. It motivated me to honor him with the trust and sacrifice he had made for me. I can imagine that was also how Onesimus felt.

When you recognize the tremendous gift that Jesus has given you by becoming your pledge for good, your surety, your cosigner for righteousness, your life is transformed from self-fulfillment to one of gratitude.

Devotional: What Gratitude Looks Like

So what does gratitude look like?

1. First, gratitude looks like anticipation: "My eyes fail from seeking Your salvation and Your righteous word" (Psalm 119:123 NKJV).

Imagine having such an understanding of grace and such confidence in the righteousness of Jesus that has been transferred to us that you look forward to the day of judgment.

Instead of fearing judgment, you look forward to it with anticipation, seeing it as the closing of a deal that you know will work out in your favor because your cosigner is there with you with your debt paid in full.

Having gratitude for your cosigner makes you long to see him. Once I got my 1986 Shelby Charger, the first thing I wanted to do was drive to Jacksonville, Florida, to visit my granddad. I was so excited to see him, I got stopped twice for speeding and ended up with one ticket and one warning.

2. Second, gratitude looks like wisdom: "Deal with Your servant according to Your mercy, and teach me Your statutes. I am Your servant; give me understanding, that I may know Your testimonies" (Psalm 119:124–125 NKJV).

The responsibility of living with the benefits of someone else's good name—that is, the righteousness of Christ—changes the way you interact with the world around you.

You become less addicted to the world, and your decisions change. You start making choices based on God's Word rather than the passions of your flesh. You're driven to know more about your cosigner—why He would do such a thing for you—through His Word.

3. Third, gratitude looks like changed values: "It is time for You to act, O LORD, for they have regarded Your law as void. Therefore I love Your commandments more than gold, yes, than fine gold! Therefore all Your precepts concerning all things I consider to be right; I hate every false way" (Psalm 119:126–128 NKJV).

Once you understand the cost for Jesus to cosign for you, it transforms your value system. Your gratitude for Him manifests itself daily in how you spend your time, how you spend your money, what you talk about in conversation and on social media. The percentage of your conversation that focuses on what Jesus has done for you increases as you gain more knowledge and understanding of the cost paid for pledge for good.

As we continue to grow in knowledge and love for God's Word, we will also continue to grow in knowledge and love of Jesus Christ, our cosigner. May we live lives of gratitude characterized by anticipation, wisdom, and changed values as we confidently rejoice in the knowledge our debt of sin has been paid.

Chapter Sixteen Questions

Question: Have you ever cosigned for someone or had someone cosign for you? What insights did that experience give you into the idea of Jesus as your cosigner?

_____

_____

_____

_____

_____

_____

_____

_____

_____

_____

_____

Question: Do you approach God with boldness and confidence in your right standing with Him? If not, what hinders you from having this freedom? How can you better understand and live out the truths of your justification before God?

_____

_____

_____

_____

_____

_____

_____

_____

_____

_____

Question: Is your life characterized by gratitude for what Christ has done for you? How is your gratitude manifested in anticipation of seeing Him face to face? What is the difference between a life of gratitude vs. trying to pay back Jesus through religious activities and rituals?

_____

_____

_____

_____

_____

_____

_____

_____

_____

_____

_____

_____

Action: Spend some time reflecting on your own salvation testimony and what Jesus did in paying and cancelling out your entire sin debt before God. Find a song or verse that expresses your heart of praise toward Him for this incredible gift, and spend time in worship.

Chapter Sixteen Notes

CHAPTER SEVENTEEN

Pe—Panting for God's Word

Jocelyn Brubaker, a friend of ours, is a well-known baking blogger. Her blog is called *Inside BruCrew Life*.[63] Last year she made a vanilla bean apple cheesecake for my wife's birthday. It was creamy and smooth, with the just the right mixture of sweetness and tartness. Even though it was probably at least a thousand calories a bite, it didn't taste heavy. It seemed like you could eat it forever and never get enough, like it couldn't possibly be bad for you.

This example was fresh in my mind as I studied this seventeenth stanza, titled "Pe," which describes David's passion for God's Word. It describes and defines where we should be at this point in our study of Psalm 119.

*Your testimonies are **wonderful**; therefore my soul keeps them. The **entrance** of Your words gives **light**; it gives understanding to the simple. I opened my mouth and **panted**, for I longed for Your commandments. Look upon me and*

> be merciful to me, as Your custom is toward those who love
> Your name. Direct my steps by Your word, and let no iniq-
> uity have dominion over me. Redeem me from the
> oppression of man, that I may keep Your precepts. Make
> Your face shine upon Your servant, and teach me Your
> statutes. Rivers of water run down from my eyes, because
> men do not keep Your law.
>
> **—Psalm 119:129–136** *(NKJV, emphasis added)*

> *When I approach God's Word as an academic, uninspir-*
> *ing habit, the results are occasional "runs" of*
> *spirituality and spiritual highs. To me, that's not true*
> *spiritual growth and fellowship with God. Real spiritual*
> *growth requires a passionate love relationship with the*
> *Word of God.*
>
> **—From Joe's journal**

If you've truly been given the gift of faith, what David describes is where you will eventually be with God's Word. Loving God's Word is a direct result of the gift of the faith, and faith never fails to save or transform.

Historical: Hebrew Word Study

The psalmist was a man trying his best to describe in human terms what God's Word did for his heart. He was a liar, an adulterer, and a murderer, making for an interesting dichotomy—a ridiculous sinner who was in love with God's Word.

> *I opened my mouth and panted, for I longed for your com-*
> *mandments.*
>
> **—Psalm 119:131** *(NKJV)*

Let's dig a little deeper into the original Hebrew that the psalmist uses to describe God's Word. The word translated "wonderful" in verse 129 is the Hebrew *pele,* which refers to a miracle or a marvelous thing.[64] Here, the miracle is God's act of redemption. The psalmist considered God's testimonies to be an amazing, perplexing, miraculous act of redemption.

In verse 130, the Hebrew word translated as "entrance" is *pethach,* which means "a grand opening."[65] The Lexham English Bible translates this same word as "unfolding, or a breathtaking reveal." The psalmist was essentially saying that when God's Word was revealed to him, it took his breath away and gave him new insights into the world.

Also in verse 130, the word translated as "light" is the Hebrew *uwr,* meaning "light, particularly coming from the East"[66]—the break of glorious day, set on fire so that it reveals flaws. This word is dynamic—bright and shining and brilliant. It is also, however, a light that reveals flaws. It can cause discomfort, maybe even pain, but it's also a light that gives direction to those who are simple, who have not yet grown in wisdom.

Lastly, the Hebrew word translated as "panted" in verse 131 is *sha'aph,* which means "to inhale eagerly, to desire, to devour, to swallow up."[67] The psalmist wanted to swallow up and consume God's Word the way my family and I wanted to devour all of Jocelyn's cheesecake at once.

With these words, David described how his intense passion and desire for the Word of God affects him. He had such a passion for God's Word that this was what was taking place in his heart.

First, his longing for God's Word had a *spiritual* impact: "Your testimonies are wonderful; therefore my soul keeps them" (Psalm 119:129 NKJV).

Second, his longing had an *intellectual* impact: "The

entrance of Your words gives light; it gives understanding to the simple. I opened my mouth and panted, for I longed for Your commandments" (Psalm 119:130 NKJV).

Third, his longing had a *physical* impact: "I opened my mouth and panted, for I longed you're your commandments" (Psalm 119:131 NKJV).

There was a yearning, a feeling in his gut when it came to hearing and learning God's truth. Its majesty took his breath away.

Throughout David's life, we see him constantly migrating back to God's Word. It was the dominant force in his life—more than relationships, money, power, or sex. Even during his greatest failures, his heart always panted for God's Word and ran back to the truth.

God's Word was David's passion, and he articulates this in a way that is both ingeniously simple and all-encompassing: his soul, his mind, and his body are all impacted by his love for God's Word.

Theological: The Impact of Panting

The psalmist said he panted for the Word of God (v. 131). He longed for it. His mouth watered for it because he understood God's Word is so much more than a book. He craved the way God saw him and spoke to him through that book. When your hunger for the Word of God gets to this point, it's tied to an understanding of God's grace, mercy, and redemption.

Once you understand God's Word isn't a list of rules, but rather a story of redemption, grace, mercy, and reconnection to the Father, you can't help but love it. The result is a level of intimacy with God's Word that creates the following behaviors:

1. Panting for God's Word creates confidence: "Look upon me and be merciful to me, as Your custom is toward those who love Your name" (Psalm 119:132 NKJV).

The psalmist wanted God to look at him. Compare that to what Adam and Eve did when they sinned—they tried to cover themselves up (Genesis 3:8–11). David, however, asked God to turn and look at him and love him, which is God's customary habit with those who love Him.

Confidence in mercy builds a relationship with God and His Word that won't be ashamed of what His Word might tell you. You are not afraid of God looking at you because you know His grace has been applied to you.

God gives mercy to His children through redemption, and we learn about this grace and redemption through His Word. God's Word becomes more precious to us as we discover we can boldly go to Him and pray for mercy, fully expecting Him to impart it. We can be confident we will not be ashamed when He turns His attention to us.

This confidence brings about that kind of prayer Paul talked about in Philippians 4:6: "Do not be anxious about anything, but in everything by prayer and supplication with thanksgiving let your requests be made known to God."

Hebrews 4:16 encourages us: "Let us then with confidence draw near to the throne of grace, that we may receive mercy and find grace to help in time of need."

2. Panting for God's Word creates consistency: "Direct my steps by Your word, and let no iniquity have dominion over me. Redeem me from the oppression of man, that I may keep Your precepts. Make Your face shine upon Your servant, and teach me Your statutes" (Psalm 119:133–135 NKJV).

The psalmist asked God to keep him steady and consistent in his obedience to God's Word. Consistency in God's Word is born out of inspiration, not restriction, compulsion, or guilt. You don't become a good follower of God's Word because you feel bad about who you are or because you're motivated enough to be religious. That's not where consistency comes from.

Some people approach the Word of God out of compulsion. They see it as a task that results in occasional runs of spirituality, but that is not consistent spiritual growth and fellowship with God. Compare that with seeing the unfolding of God's Word as miraculous and breathtaking. That's the difference between compulsion and inspiration.

When God's Word becomes refreshing to you, it creates a lifestyle of inspired, consistent living, a lifestyle that makes Heavenly Dad smile. I often like to pray that Heavenly Dad will help me to make Him smile. It seems impossible, given all the sin in my life, but I'm not afraid to let God look at me because I understand grace.

> *Jesus answered him, "If anyone loves me, he will keep my word, and my Father will love him, and we will come to him and make our home with him. Whoever does not love me does not keep my words. And the word that you hear is not mine but the Father's who sent me."*
> —*John 14:23-24*

Notice that Jesus doesn't say, "If anyone is afraid of me, he will keep My Word." It's anyone who loves Him—anyone who pants for Him.

3. Panting for God's Word creates compassion: "Rivers of water run down from my eyes, because men do not keep Your law" (Psalm 119:136 NKJV).

The psalmist was not weeping over some personal hardship here, such as Saul trying to kill him, the death of the son born to him through his adultery with Bathsheba, or the Philistines preparing to attack. He was crying because he was distressed because God's Word was being disregarded.

If we are truly in tune with God's Word, we will be grieved when we see His Word being disregarded because we know what the tragic outcome will be: a life not connected to Heavenly Dad through His Word. Paul gives a great example of this grieving:

> *I am speaking the truth in Christ—I am not lying; my conscience bears me witness in the Holy Spirit—that I have great sorrow and unceasing anguish in my heart. For I could wish that I myself were accursed and cut off from Christ for the sake of my brothers, my kinsmen according to the flesh.*
>
> **—Romans 9:1–3**

Paul's heart was so grieved that his fellow Jews had rejected Christ and were going to face judgment that he wished he could be cut off from Christ if it meant they could be connected. (This is a slight callback to what we learned about *surety* in the last chapter.)

When was the last time you wept over a concern that wasn't your own? When did you last feel pain and grief for a person who was disobedient and out of God's will? This is one result of panting for God's Word. You want people to understand how much better life lived in grace can be, and your heart aches for them because they just don't get it. You wish you could help them, and your tears flow.

Devotional: It's Time

Every believer should have the goal of getting to this level of intimacy and inspiration with God's Word. That's been the entire point of our journey through Psalm 119. I encourage you to take a moment and evaluate where you are. I challenge you to take this concept to heart.

When I was in ninth grade, a youth pastor taught me there are three stages in a person's relationship with God's Word.

1. The first stage is medicine. It tastes bad, but you must force it down because you know you need it to get better. Maybe your relationship with God's Word is  like that right now. You're not exactly panting after it because it doesn't taste very good.

2. The second stage is dry cereal. It's bearable and nutritious, but it's dry. Sometimes God's Word can be a little dry. You wish you had some milk or maybe a  spoonful of sugar. It's not medicine, but it still takes effort to consume it.

3. The third stage is peaches and cream. It's smooth, sweet, and tasty. You're salivating before you even get it into your mouth. You pant for it.

Which stage are you in right now? Honestly, at this point, I'm probably at dry cereal, along with probably about seventy percent of Christians. But I've tasted peaches and cream at other moments in my life, and I want to do so again.

I want to challenge you to face the stage you're in today. If you're not at peaches and cream, ask God to help you get there. Ask Him to help you develop the type of connection to His Word that David had. At some point in your life, you should be able to say with integrity that you're at peaches and cream. You should be able to identify with the words of the psalmist:

> *How sweet are Your words to my taste, sweeter than honey to my mouth!*
>
> **—Psalm 119:103** (NKJV)

We have five stanzas remaining in Psalm 119, and they will describe the things that keep us away from peaches and cream. My desire is you would learn how to pant for God's Word, and I pray that would be your desire as well.

Chapter Seventeen Questions

Question: Do you have a true passion for God's Word? What spiritual, intellectual, and/or physical impact does it have on your life? Would you describe your relationship with the Bible as bitter medicine, dry cereal, or peaches and cream? How can you increase in your passion and affection for God's Word?

_____

_____

_____

_____

_____

_____

_____

_____

_____

Question: Consistency in God's Word is born out of inspiration, not restriction, compulsion, or guilt. Rules and guilt can get results, so why are they ultimately dangerous motivators? Have you observed Christian leaders using compulsion or guilt to coerce people into studying the Bible? What can a believer do who does not *feel* inspired to read the Word but who wants to have a grace-based passion for the Scriptures?

_____

_____

_____

_____

_____

_____

_____

_____

_____

_____

_____

Question: Where do you grieve over the disregard of God's Word and resulting brokenness in others' lives? When did Jesus display this attitude of compassionate sorrow?

_____

_____

_____

_____

_____

_____

_____

_____

_____

_____

_____

Action: Make or purchase a special treat to share with friends or family. As you all enjoy this delicious food, talk about the sweet and precious truths of God's Word He is revealing to each of you. Encourage one another in developing a greater passion for the Bible and pray that it will be sweeter to your souls than the best dessert is to your palette!

_____

_____

_____

_____

_____

_____

_____

_____

Chapter Seventeen Notes

CHAPTER EIGHTEEN

Tsadhe—Pursuing Righteousness

My motivation for loving God's Word should not be so I can "act righteous." My attempts at righteousness don't make God smile. It is my gratitude for HIS righteousness inserted into my life that makes Him smile. Any attempt at self-righteousness is feeble and motivated by arrogance. The acknowledgment of God's righteousness within me is the key.

—From Joe's journal

Many people are intimidated by the idea of pursuing righteousness. It seems like a far-off, untouchable concept or religious fantasy, a desert road with no road signs, no rest stops, no gas stations, and no destination in sight. The journey is daunting, and we know before we even start that we'll never arrive.

Wouldn't it be easier if we could just ignore righteousness and pretend the concept doesn't exist? Even though we want to be righteous, we know we can't get there on our own, and it becomes an emotional, spiritual burden.

For some reason, the unrighteous, murderous, adulterous psalmist sang about it. What in the world does David know about righteousness? He discusses this concept in the eighteenth stanza of Psalm 119, titled "Tsadhe."

Righteous are you, O Lᴏʀᴅ, and *upright* are your judgments. Your testimonies, which You have commanded, are righteous and very faithful. My zeal has consumed me, because my enemies have forgotten your words. Your word is very pure; therefore Your servant loves it. I am small and despised, yet I do not forget your precepts. Your righteousness is an everlasting righteousness, and Your law is truth. Trouble and anguish have overtaken me, yet Your commandments are my delights. The righteousness of Your testimonies is everlasting; give me understanding, and I shall live.

—Psalm 119:137–144 (NKJV, emphasis added)

Historical: Hebrew Word Study

Let's dig into the original Hebrew of this stanza so that we can better understand the righteousness the psalmist was speaking of. The word translated as "righteous" in verse 137 is the Hebrew *tsaddiyq,* which means "just or lawful."[68] The Hebrew word translated as "upright" in that same verse is *yashar,* meaning "straight"—both literally and figuratively.[69]

The psalmist describes righteousness in two different ways.

He first gives a literary reference to God's righteousness, portraying it as a book of law. He then follows it with a geometric reference portraying God's righteousness as a straight line. Not only is God's righteousness written out perfectly, but it is also a straight, unwavering line. There's one image for people who see things from a literary, word-based perspective and one image for people who think in more visual and artistic terms.

The Hebrew word translated as "commanded" in verse

138 is *tsavah,* meaning "to appoint or send a messenger, to declare or set the record straight."[70] The psalmist was saying that God had appointed someone and something to declare what righteousness is. The psalmist knew where righteousness comes from and that only God is righteous. He also understood the appointed messenger of this righteousness is the actual Word of God. God's Word is the extension, the declaring body of righteousness.

> *In the beginning was the Word, and the Word was with God, and the Word was God.*
>
> **—John 1:1**

Jesus Christ is the Word of God. The Word is the expression of the mind of God and His character. That's why the psalmist declared God is righteous, and God's Word is righteous as well.

David's authority on righteousness, his ability to write a song on the subject in this album, came from what he learned from the Word of God. It did not come from personal success in being righteous but from what he read about righteousness from the messenger of righteousness, which is God's Word: His law, His truth, and His Son. It is only because of this that an unrighteousness king could write expertly about righteousness.

Theological: Righteous Confidence

David simultaneously and majestically describes two things about God's Word. It's an artistic dichotomy. First, he showed humility about his own righteousness. He acknowledged he was "small and despised" (v. 141) and "trouble and anguish" had found him out (v. 143). He described righteousness by making it clear he was the opposite of righteousness.

Second, while recognizing he was as far from right-eousness as he could ever be, David was still confident. He describes how a man who knows he is not righteous himself lives with all the benefits that come with right-eousness. Even though he was pitiful and lowly, he lived as though he was not. It would be like us living as though we have Bill Gates' money. That's how far we are from having our own righteousness.

This confidence David had in his God-given righteous-ness manifested itself in different ways:

1. David had confidence while surrounded: "My zeal has consumed me, because my enemies have forgotten your words. Your word is very pure; therefore Your serv-ant loves it. I am small and despised, yet I do not forget your precepts" (Psalm 119:139–141 NKJV).

The psalmist describes two ways he is surrounded by unrighteousness: the unrighteous people around him and the unrighteousness within him. Everywhere he looked, he was surrounded. He was zealous for righteousness, but he also realized he was troubled and despised.

The psalmist had the confidence to live as though he was righteous even though there were two glaring sources of unrighteousness that permeated every area of his life. He describes a man who knows he is not righteous himself yet lives as though he is. He declared confidence in God's righteous words, not his own righteous deeds. He was therefore able to have confidence in his righteousness even in a sea of unrighteousness.

2. David had confidence regarding eternity: "Your righteousness is an everlasting righteousness, and Your law is truth" (Psalm 119:142 NKJV*)*.

Look at John 17:17, where Jesus prays, "Sanctify them in the truth; your word is truth." He asked God to set His followers apart and make them righteous.

The psalmist recognized this and could live with con-fidence in eternity, despite being surrounded by unrighteousness. By God's grace through faith, the psalmist was made righteous and sanctified, set apart. Sanctification is the process of being conformed to God's righteousness. This isn't accomplished by religion, discipline, or to-do lists, but through truth. God's Word is truth, and to be sanctified by it, you must spend time with it.

It's not about an outward conformity to people's expectations but about an inward change of our very nature. We tend to want to start from the outside and work our way in because the outside is easier to change. We do a good job, perhaps especially as American Christians, putting icing on a sewage cake. We put on that smile and act like we live as good Christians, but that appearance hides the filth of our sin and thoughts on the inside. Occasionally, life scrapes off some of the icing, revealing the mess underneath, and we fall into shame.

By contrast, the psalmist focused on the fact that spending time with God's Word was truly sanctifying him. We are made righteous according to God's standards by the truth of His Word.

Do you want to stop being ashamed of who you were in the past, who you are in the present, or who you might become in the future? Spend some time in God's Word. We can face eternity with confidence and peace because we know our righteousness is about God's work, not ours. It's an inward change, not an outward conformity.

3. David had confidence during failure: "Trouble and anguish have overtaken me, yet Your commandments are my delights. The righteousness of Your testimonies is everlasting; give me understanding, and I shall live" (Psalm 119:143–144 NKJV).

Why are we so often prisoners to guilt and shame about our past? Why are we enslaved by regrets and failures? Because we don't understand what righteousness really is or where it comes from. It's absolutely foolish to think we could ever achieve righteousness by doing things a certain way.

We tend to think if we had just made better decisions in the past or if we could go back and change the things we did wrong, we would be righteous. This is a lie from the enemy. It doesn't line up with Scripture. On our own, we were not righteous in the past, we aren't righteous in the present, and we certainly won't be righteous in the future!

> As it is written: "None is righteous, no, not one; no one understands; no one seeks for God. All have turned aside; together they have become worthless; no one does good, not even one."
> **—Romans 3:10–12**

In these verses from Romans, Paul was quoting David:

> The LORD looks down from heaven on the children of men, to see if there are any who understand, who seek God. They have all turned aside, they have together become corrupt; there is none who does good, no, not one.
> **—Psalm 14:2–3** (NKJV)

You can try as hard as you want to measure up on your own—as a spouse, a parent, a friend, an employee, and a Christ-follower—but you will never succeed.

The fact is, the more we take stock of our own righteousness, the more we realize what colossal failures we are in this department. Yet in spite of knowing all that, David escaped the prison of shame by embracing God's righteousness as his own.

How could he be so audacious? Who did he think he was? David's audacity comes from one place: a love affair with God's Word. That really is the secret.

Living Within Righteousness

You've heard the phrase *living in righteousness*. I want you to take that phrase, crumple it up, and throw it in the trash can. Instead, try a new phrase: *living within righteousness*. It's a new perspective. Living in righteousness seems to rely on human effort, but living within righteousness means we are operating within the righteousness of Christ, and all its benefits. We recognize our righteousness is not our own, but instead we live in the wide place created by the righteousness of Christ. He has achieved what we never could achieve on our own. We have been set free to roam within God's righteousness on our behalf.

> Indeed, I count everything as loss because of the surpassing worth of knowing Christ Jesus my Lord. For his sake I have suffered the loss of all things and count them as rubbish, in order that I may gain Christ and be found in him, not having a righteousness of my own that comes from the law, but that which comes through faith in Christ, the righteousness from God that depends on faith.
> —*Philippians 3:8–9*

Some of you have experienced "the loss of all things"—jobs, family, friends, relationships. You look back and think there were times you had it all. But really, you had nothing! When you understand that righteousness comes from God, then the losses you have experienced, instead of producing shame, will remind you of how thankful you should be that you can live within righteousness, not through it.

Just like David, Paul was able to do two things.

1. First, he embraced his failures. Paul had it all, but instead of despairing over these things he had lost, he saw his loss as the path to life, redemption, and restoration—the ability to live within the righteousness of God.

2. Second, Paul lived within Christ, the source of the righteousness we so miserably fail to achieve on our own. Without our failures in attaining righteousness, we would never turn to live within the true source. We would continue to think it was possible to attain righteousness on our own. But the failures are blessings that drive us to go where righteousness truly resides, and that's within a relationship with Christ through God's Word.

David and Paul were both colossal failures at personal righteousness, yet they reached this place of confidence and freedom because they spent time in the Word of God, which taught them to live within God's righteousness.

It's important to note that both men found this confidence in the Old Testament. Paul did not have a New Testament. He learned about righteousness from studying the law. Paul recognized the importance of righteousness so much that he quoted David's words several times in his epistles. The New Testament draws heavily on the Old Testament.

Like Paul and David, if you are in God's Word, you learn what it means to live within the righteousness of Jesus, and it miraculously sanctifies and transforms you. We do this by living lives that seek to be obedient to what we learn in the Word of God. That's part of the process of sanctification. This is not an excuse to sin without repercussions.

> *What shall we say then? Are we to continue in sin that grace may abound? By no means! How can we who died to sin still live in it?*
>
> **—Romans 6:1–2**

This is not saying, "I can do whatever I want because I'm within the righteousness of Jesus." We are called to live with gratitude within this righteousness.

Devotional: Embracing the Righteousness of Christ

Today, right now, is the day I want you to stop fretting over your past failures and your personal righteousness. It's time to be like the adulterous, murderous, deceitful psalmist and live within the righteousness of Jesus—even as the enemy tries to yank you out of it, reminding you that you were a failure, are a failure, and will be a failure.

It's time to recognize you have been covered by the righteousness of God Himself through His Son. Every time you give into shame and guilt, you're refusing to live within righteousness. Instead, you willingly choose to drown in the sewage of your own insufficiency. Instead of embracing the righteousness God has given you, you're sulking over your personal unrighteousness. By spending time in God's Word, you will come to recognize the righteousness God has given you is now your own and respond with gratitude.

As you fall in love with God's Word, you will learn God sees you within the righteousness of Christ. I know that can be hard to believe and even harder to embrace, but when Heavenly Dad looks at us, instead of seeing our failures, shame and guilt, all He sees is Jesus.

> *I will greatly rejoice in the LORD, my soul shall be joyful in my God; for he has clothed me with the garments of salvation, he has covered me with the robe of righteousness, as a bridegroom decks himself with ornaments, and as a bride adorns herself with her jewels.*
> *—Isaiah 61:10 (NKJV)*

That certainly doesn't sound like guilt and shame! Christ died for us so that we could be clothed within His righteousness and be reconciled to a righteous God. It is

His righteousness alone that counts. Praise God that He is righteous, because that's why we can live within His righteousness!

It's also the reason you no longer must be enslaved to the unrighteous past, the miserable failure of a present, or the hopeless future. You can have hope because you are within the righteousness of Christ.

WORKBOOK

Chapter Eighteen Questions

Question: What images and ideas come to mind when you hear the word *righteousness*? Whom do you think of? Are you confident calling yourself a *righteous person*? Why or why not?

_____

_____

_____

_____

_____

_____

_____

_____

_____

_____

_____

Question: When and how have you confused a righteousness of outward conformity with one of inward change? When and how have you tried to make yourself righteous instead of accepting and living within Christ's righteousness for you?

_____

_____

_____

_____

_____

_____

_____

_____

_____

_____

Question: How can memories of past failures, shame, guilt, and sin be transformed into reminders to embrace and rejoice in Christ's righteousness on your behalf?

_____

_____

_____

_____

_____

_____

_____

_____

_____

_____

_____

_____

Action: Choose a verse that speaks of Christ's imputed righteousness (e.g., 2 Corinthians 5:21 or Romans 8:1–4) to memorize. When you start to be pulled into regrets about the past, shame about the present, or fears about the future, let this verse be your reminder that you can be confident in the righteousness you have before God.

Chapter Eighteen Notes

CHAPTER NINETEEN

Qoph—Hope When Times Get Dark

Think back to the most painful moments of your life. We experience pain for all kinds of reasons—betrayal, personal failure, illness, natural disaster, etc. In your darkest moments, in the deepest, darkest part of your pain, where did your heart run to? What did your mind gravitate toward?

Here are a few of the darkest times in my life that I wrote about in my journal and the Scriptures that comforted me:

Betrayal: While I was in college I was betrayed by a close friend in ways you can't Imagine. All I wanted was for God to take this pain away so I could get back to focusing on His Word.

False accusations: When false accusations against my character were made while on staff at a church. It was so hard to listen to these people telling me how awful I was. I knew they were wrong, and I had evidence they were wrong, but no one seemed to care. I turned to

Matthew 5:10–11.

Unspeakable grief: When we lost our daughter in a car accident, I turned to 1 Corinthians 9:19–23. This Scripture became a theme of my ministry going forward as I sought to pattern ministry after the character my daughter displayed in her life.

Rejection: When I was callously rejected by a friend I needed desperately during the first few months of our grief over Sarah. He said to me, "I don't want you here anymore. You're too much of a burden." That was heartbreakingly painful. I turned to Psalm 142. I read that psalm eight times a day.

Failure: When part of the ministry we started in memory of Sarah failed, I felt I had let Sarah's memory down, and I ran to God's Word. I turned to Jeremiah 29:11.

—From Joe's journal

Imagine if the first place our hearts ran to in dark times was the Word of God. Here in the nineteenth stanza, titled "Qoph," the psalmist expresses his passion for God's Word in the absolute worst moments of his existence:

*I **cry** out with my whole heart; **hear me**, O LORD! I will keep Your statutes. I cry out to You; save me, and I will keep Your testimonies. I rise before the dawning of the morning, and cry for help; I hope in Your word. My eyes are awake through the night watches, that I may meditate on Your word. Hear my voice according to Your lovingkindness; O LORD, revive me according to Your justice. They draw near who follow after wickedness; they are far from Your law. You are near, O LORD, and all Your commandments are truth. Concerning Your testimonies, I have known of old that You have founded them forever.*

—Psalm 119:145–152 (NKJV, emphasis added)

Historical: Hebrew Word Study

Let's dig into the original Hebrew of this stanza to get a better understanding of David's dark times. The Hebrew word translated as "cry" in verse 145 is *qara*. The psalmist uses this same Hebrew word again in verse 146.

This is the only time in Psalm 119 where the psalmist uses the exact same word twice, and he uses a word that has two meanings. This is so deep and so artistically complex that I want you to understand the beauty of it.

The first use of this word is "to cry, utter a loud sound."[71] We can infer by the context of this stanza it could be the result of a painful experience, perhaps one that was unsolicited and without warning. It's the kind of experience you don't see coming—it just runs you over like a semi-truck.

The context of the stanza clearly indicates the psalmist's loud cry is directed specifically to draw the attention of his God for help. The psalmist experienced tremendous pain he didn't ask for, and he cried aloud at his God about it. He uses the same word twice to give deep color to exactly what his cry was and to whom it was directed.

The word translated as "hear me" in verse 145 is the Hebrew *anah,* which means "to heed, to pay attention, to respond." Specifically, it means "to sing, to shout, to testify or announce."[72] The psalmist was going through ridiculous, unsolicited pain, and he accosted God with his words in hopes that God would pay close attention and respond to him.

Lastly, the Hebrew word translated as "save" in verse 146 is *yasha,* meaning "to be free, to be safe, to avenge or defend, to preserve, to rescue, to be given a victory."[73] This is the other thing the psalmist wanted God to do. He not only wanted God to listen to him, he wanted God to save him, perhaps even avenge him.

David's Dark Times

Note how the psalmist promised to respond if God heard him and saved him. He promised that, even during his darkest times, he would keep God's statutes and observe His testimonies (vv. 145–146). The psalmist wanted relief from his horrible pain so he could remove what was distracting him from obedience. He wanted to embrace and follow the Word of God.

David asked God to rescue him, to save him, to give him His attention so he could turn his attention back to hearing God's Word. He desired relief so that he could be obedient. He wanted to live in gratitude for what God had done for him, to remember he had been clothed in righteousness. The psalmist believes his pain is a distraction from what he wants to focus on.

Before you can properly appreciate the emotion in this stanza, you need to understand some history about David. Here is some background on some of David's most famous psalms that he wrote and relied on when times were dark. We know this information because of the titles included at the beginning of each psalm.

- Psalm 3: written when David fled from his son Absalom.

- Psalm 7: written when David was slandered by someone who wanted to take him down.

- Psalm 34: written when David acted insane in front of a pagan king to escape death.

- Psalm 51: written when David was confronted by the prophet Nathan after his adultery with Bathsheba and his murder of her husband, Uriah.

- Psalm 52: written when David was betrayed by

Doeg the Edomite, who told Saul where David was hiding.

- Psalm 57: written when David was hiding in a cave from Saul, who was trying to kill him.

- Psalm 59: written when Saul sent men to watch David's house to kill him.

- Psalm 63: written when David was hiding in the wilderness.

- Psalm 140: written when David was seeking deliverance from evil men.

- Psalm 142: written when David was hiding in a cave.

These are all examples of dark times in David's life. Can you see where he turned in those dark times? He remembered the moments he had with God, and he remembered God's promises in the law, the Torah. These things inspired him so much he was able to write incredible songs out of his painful experiences.

David's connection to God and His Word created an instinct to turn to God's truth in the darkest of times. When his heart was broken, he turned to God's Word. When his heart was grieving, he turned to God's Word. When he faced his own guilt and sinfulness, he turned to God's Word. In addition, we learn from this stanza, that he would turn to God loudly!

Theological: Heavenly Instincts

In the following verses, David provides examples of when his heart and mind would turn to God during these dark times.

1. His heart and mind would turn to God when he

couldn't sleep: "I rise before the dawning of the morning, and cry for help; I hope in Your word. My eyes are awake through the night watches, that I may meditate on Your word" (Psalm 119:147–148 NKJV).

We've all had times we were so burdened about something that we couldn't sleep. Maybe it was guilt, anxiety, injustice, or grief. We've all been there. The psalmist described those times and how, when he couldn't sleep, he thought about God's promise.

2. His heart and mind would turn to God when no one was listening to him: "Hear my voice according to Your lovingkindness; O LORD, revive me according to Your justice" (Psalm 119:149 NKJV).

When David felt alone and no one was there for him, he would cry out loudly to God.

This wasn't a religious reaction to loneliness but an emotional one, a natural migration of his heart toward God's Word. He wasn't doing this as a pastor, a scientist, or a mathematician. He was simply an emotional creature who was a wreck and feeling alone.

3. His heart and mind would turn to God when evil was near: "They draw near who follow after wickedness; they are far from Your law. You are near, O LORD, and all Your commandments are truth. Concerning Your testimonies, I have known of old that You have founded them forever" (Psalm 119:150–152 NKJV).

When David felt trapped or cornered, he rested in the knowledge that God was near, and His Word was reliable. This was the result of learning God's promises and seeing them fulfilled time after time—before the darkness, before the betrayal, before the loneliness. Knowing the promises of God beforehand helped him remember the times when God's Word had come through for him, often in dramatic fashion.

This emotional, passionate, extremely flawed man wrote psalms that have resonated with people for generations. I've read Psalm 51, when David was confronted about Bathsheba and Uriah, probably about four thousand times in my life. David's psalms have had a tremendous impact on so many people.

Falling in Love with God in Dark Times

The best times to fall in love with God's Word are during the hardest times of our lives. When we are experiencing the depths of pain and sorrow, our experiences with God's Word can be stunning and supernatural. This is not theory. As I explained earlier in the chapter, I have experienced it myself.

As I get older and think more about my own frailty and mortality, I have realized the most precious times I've had with God's Word and with Heavenly Dad have been during the worst times of my life. During those times I couldn't help but cry out loudly to God to gain His attention. I can remember the Scriptures I turned to during those times—when I couldn't sleep, when no one else would listen, when I felt evil was close by—more than all the others I've ever read or preached on.

I have spent many times with God's Word, but those are the times I remember and cherish. The moments my loud cries were desperate to gain His attention. I remember those passages, what they tasted like as I read them, the specific truths that pacified my anxiety, my anger, my ambivalence, my sorrow, and my bitterness. Those are my most precious journal entries—not the ones where I got the job I wanted, not the ones about planting the church where I currently serve as pastor, but the ones about the darkest times in my life.

If I had been a prolific songwriter like David, I would've written songs about them. Instead, I wrote sermons about them, fulfilling Paul's encouragement to us:

Blessed be the God and Father of our Lord Jesus Christ, the Father of mercies and God of all comfort, who comforts us in all our affliction, so that we may be able to comfort those who are in any affliction, with the comfort with which we ourselves are comforted by God.

—2 Corinthians 1:3–4

Devotional: Prepare for Dark Times Now

Think about how the echoes of David's darkest times have been a comfort to so many. I'm so glad David's life was hard! It's made the worst moments of my life and those in the lives of so many others bearable. But you won't know that if you don't spend time in God's Word.

William Shakespeare was an incredibly gifted writer and an amazing communicator. He might be one of the most famous people who ever walked the face of the earth. He, too, was familiar with the comfort God offers to those who are going through dark times.

Now God be praised; that to believing souls/Gives light in darkness, comfort in despair![74]
—King Henry, *King Henry VI*, Part II

Whether you've yet to experience dark times or have experienced so many that you've lost count, I encourage you to spend more time in God's Word. Get ready now so that when dark times inevitably come your way, your heart and mind will already be trained to run to the truth that won't let you down. Your heart and mind will cry aloud with confidence and raw emotion to your God for His attention.

WORKBOOK

Chapter Nineteen Questions

Question: Looking back over your life, what have been the most painful times or darkest moments that you have faced? During any of these times did you find comfort in God's Word? What verses or passages impacted you? Describe the difference between a season of suffering where you ran to God's Word for hope and comfort vs. one where you did not?

_____

_____

_____

_____

_____

_____

_____

_____

_____

Question: The psalmist experienced tremendous pain he didn't ask for, and he cried aloud at his God about it. Are you able to take your anger, grief, trauma, and pain to God in an authentic way, or do you feel you have to make all your prayers *nice*? How might the level of genuineness expressed by the psalmist help grow your relationship with God and give you strength in difficult times?

_____

_____

_____

_____

_____

_____

_____

_____

_____

_____

_____

Question: When was the last time you couldn't sleep because of anxiety or grief? What are some ways people typically deal with insomnia? How might these other ways cause you to miss the opportunity for a deep and precious connection with God?

_____

_____

_____

_____

_____

_____

_____

_____

_____

_____

_____

_____

Action: Are you ready for dark times when they come? Are your heart and mind trained to run to the truth of God's Word, to call out to Him loudly? Scan the book of Psalms over the next few months and start a list of several psalms that speak to your heart. Make note of the various difficulties that the psalmist faced and how God spoke to him through each one. Create or find a list that gives common difficulties (loneliness, loss, betrayal, fear) and Bible passages for dealing with each one.

_____

_____

_____

_____

_____

_____

_____

_____

Chapter Nineteen Notes

CHAPTER TWENTY

Resh—Loving the Law

My case has been pleaded before the judge by the only advocate who could ever do it effectively. I have been redeemed and exonerated from a condition that was hopeless, horrifying, and helpless. My advocate was, and continues to be, Jesus Christ.
—From Joe's journal

We like laws when they protect us from criminals, vindicate us in a lawsuit, or punish someone we're convinced is truly guilty. When we personally face a judge or are accused of breaking a law, however, it gives us a queasy feeling of uncertainty.

Even when we like man's law—because it rules in our favor—none of us would choose to write songs about it. Just like man's law, many people see God's law, His Word, as something that constricts and condemns us. They see it as a list of dos and don'ts that judge us.

It's hard to embrace God's Word when all you see is its declaration of how bad you are. We struggle with falling in love with God's Word when we don't see it as the path of life, mercy, and redemption. Yet that is exactly what the psalmist expressed in this stanza—how much he loved God's Word and why.

In this twentieth stanza, titled "Resh," David expresses his love affair with the Word of God. He masterfully and poetically combines the ideas of law, love, and life and describes them in the context of his relationship with the Word of God.

> *Consider my affliction and deliver me, for I do not forget Your law. Plead my cause and redeem me; revive me according to Your word. Salvation is far from the wicked, for they do not seek Your statutes. Great are Your tender mercies, O LORD; revive me according to Your judgments. Many are my persecutors and my enemies, yet I do not turn from Your testimonies. I see the treacherous, and am disgusted, because they do not keep Your word. Consider how I love Your precepts; revive me, O LORD, according to Your lovingkindness. The entirety of Your word is truth, and every one of Your righteous judgments endures forever.*
> *—Psalm 119:153–160 (NKJV, emphasis added)*

Historical: Hebrew Word Study

Let's dig into the original Hebrew of this passage to help us better understand the psalmist's relationship with God. The Hebrew word translated as "consider" in verse 153 is *ra'ah,* actually means "to consider."[75] The psalmist was asking God to look into something for him and make a judgment regarding it.

The word translated as "affliction," also in verse 153, is the Hebrew *oniy,* meaning "depression, misery, or trouble."[76] The psalmist wanted God to investigate and make a judgment regarding his depression, his misery, his sorrow.

In verse 153, the word translated as "deliver" is the Hebrew *chalats,* which means "to pull out, to equip for battle, to present."[77] David was asking God to be his lawyer. Since God wrote the law and judges according to the law, who better to represent David and get him off the hook regarding any charges against him?

The Hebrew word translated as "plead" and "cause" in verse 154 is *riyb*. David uses the same word twice, back to back, first as a verb and then as a noun. As a verb, *riyb* means "to defend, contend, debate, or plead."[78] As a noun, it means "a cause or a case at law."[79]

It's clear that the psalmist is describing a legal setting with a law, a lawyer, and a judge. He saw himself in a spiritual courtroom with God as his judge, God as his lawyer, and God as the author of the law that David himself has broken.

The word translated as "redeem," also in verse 154, is the Hebrew *ga'al*, which means "to redeem through kinship law, to buy back a relative's property, to purchase or ransom, to serve as redeemer or avenger."[80] David not only wanted God to plead his cause but to pay his price. This was before Jesus Christ, yet David was asking God to pay the fine, to ransom him and purchase his freedom if he was found guilty.

The psalmist asked God to plead his case and win it by actively redeeming him from it. David did not depend on his talent, his position as king, his power or wisdom, or his ability to escape judgment. Instead, he put his total trust in his lawyer and cooperated with him completely, just as we would if we were in court.

David chose to work with his lawyer, the law, and the judge, all of which were the same individual. Talk about the deck being stacked in your favor! The result was that his relationship with the truth was filled with passion, dedication, gratitude, and loyalty. It was no longer a fearful, adversarial relationship.

This gives insight into what David wrote, "Oh, how I love Your law! It is my meditation all the day" (v. 97).

Imagine being in a courtroom on trial for shoplifting and telling the judge, "Before we get started, can I just say something? I love that law against shoplifting. I can't get enough of it!"

That sounds ridiculous, right? Yet David loved God's law, even though the law itself condemned him!

Theological: How Truth Becomes Seductive

Though the word *law* can be seen in a negative light, seduction describes what happens with us and God's Word once we have been given the gift of faith. We think of lies as being seductive, but to the child of God, truth is far more seductive than the lies of the world. Once you know Jesus, a transformation takes place in your heart and life. You fall less in love with the seduction of the world and more in love with the seduction of God's Word.

That's the miracle behind God's Word, the enchanting power it has over children of grace. David describes why God's Word became irresistible in the light of his vindication according to God's promise in verse 154.

Here are some qualities of God's Word the psalmist found so attractive.

1. First, the psalmist was attracted to the ultimate mercy of the Word of God: "Salvation is far from the wicked, for they do not seek Your statutes. Great are Your tender mercies, O LORD; revive me according to Your judgments" (Psalm 119:155–156 NKJV).

Salvation was far from the wicked because they didn't follow God's statutes, but the psalmist asked God to show him mercy because His rules are great. He recognized his subservience to the rules and asked for mercy even though he violated those rules.

If you haven't experienced mercy, you likely have very little interest in God's Word. Without the taste of mercy, truth becomes restricting and condemning, representing judgment and death. Everyone wants mercy, but not everyone wants to receive it through God's Word. We want mercy on our own terms. But mercy cannot be generated on your initiative. You can't taste mercy until God feeds it to you.

Once we experience that mercy and all its benefits, we start to be seduced by the Word of God. We want to learn more about this seductive mercy we've been given. As believers, we know where to go to taste God's mercy—His Word.

2. Second, the psalmist was attracted to God's Word because of the undesirable alternative: "Many are my persecutors and my enemies, yet I do not turn from Your testimonies. I see the treacherous, and am disgusted, because they do not keep Your word" (Psalm 119:157–158 NKJV).

This is a beautiful description of how unbearable life without God's Word appears for someone who loves God's Word. The psalmist was disgusted by the prospect of life without the Word of God. The people themselves didn't disgust him, but he found their lives unappealing. He couldn't imagine living life without truth because he loved God's law.

The psalmist wanted nothing to do with that kind of life. He had been seduced by truth, not by the world. Likewise, God's Word enables us to see how dark life would be without Him and without His law.

3. Third, the psalmist was driven to understand the love contained in God's Word: "Consider how I love Your precepts; revive me, O LORD, according to Your lovingkindness" (Psalm 119:159 NKJV).

The psalmist recognized life comes from one place: the love of God.

We can't understand true love on this earth until we've experienced God's love first. His Word helps us escape the world's pathetic seduction, which is packaged as love, yet is blindly rooted in selfishness.

Without God's Word, we become susceptible to the fear, doubt, and false love of the world. However, God's Word teaches us about mercy and grace that stem from God's love for us. It teaches us about the love that comes through the work of Christ, helping us understand how to truly love others. God's Word sets us free from our fears due to our confidence in knowing that His love is more powerful than that which torments us the most.

From God's Word, we learn that true love originates in sacrifice and about the effect that sacrifice can have on the one receiving it:

> *So we have come to know and to believe the love that God has for us. God is love, and whoever abides in love abides in God, and God abides in him. By this is love perfected with us, so that we may have confidence for the day of judgment, because as he is so also are we in this world. There is no fear in love, but perfect love casts out fear. For fear has to do with punishment, and whoever fears has not been perfected in love. We love because he first loved us.*
> **—1 John 4:16–19**

4. Fourth, the psalmist was attracted to God's Word because of its perfect law: "The entirety of Your word is truth, and every one of Your righteous judgments endures forever" (Psalm 119:160 NKJV).

God's Word has always been true. It's the standard by which truth and morality are measured, even when people can't see it or don't want to admit it!

Just look at the Ten Commandments and how they are the foundation for many of our laws today (Exodus 20:2–17, Deuteronomy 5:6–21). Logic won't allow you to ignore the fact that the Ten Commandments are pretty good ideas for laws. Despite efforts throughout the ages to develop new standards of truth, they always come crumbling down because immorality causes rot within a society. Ultimately, societies realize they must gravitate back toward some sort of biblical understanding, even if they don't recognize it as biblical, otherwise they will begin a slow moral collapse that eats away at its foundation.

In God's Word, we find comfort, strength, instruction, rebuke, encouragement, and hope for our future after this life because God's perfect truth is the legal and spiritual answer to our moral dilemma as a society. Truth is the answer, not politicians, social programs, or war. God's perfect truth through mercy and grace is the enduring Word that liberates us and lays out the cause for our confidence before the Judge. This is the core reason God's Word becomes so seductive for the redeemed.

The Word of Life

Wouldn't it be great to love God's Word as much as we just described and for all those seductive reasons of truth? But here's the problem: without the gift of faith, God's Word is judgmental, restrictive, and condemning. No amount of good works you do will change that.

Faith transforms God's Word, making it comforting and inspiring. It becomes a roadmap to life instead of a decree of judgment. Jesus, the living Word, wrote the law! He's the judge in our case, and he's our lawyer and advocate.

> There is therefore now no condemnation for those who are in Christ Jesus. For the law of the Spirit of life has set you free in Christ Jesus from the law of sin and death. For God has done what the law, weakened by the flesh, could not do. By sending his own Son in the likeness of sinful flesh and for sin, he condemned sin in the flesh, in order that the righteous requirement of the law might be fulfilled in us,

who walk not according to the flesh but according to the Spirit.
—Romans 8:1–4

In Christ, the law sets us free. It doesn't condemn. In this stanza of Psalm 119, David asked three times for God to give him life (vv. 154, 156, and 159). He knew that the truth of God gave him life instead of judgment. Paul echoes this concept:

And you, who were dead in your trespasses and the uncircumcision of your flesh, God made alive together with him, having forgiven us all our trespasses, by canceling the record of debt that stood against us with its legal demands. This he set aside, nailing it to the cross.
—Colossians 2:13–14

The book of Leviticus is essentially a book of rules, describing in painstaking detail the different types of sacrifices that had to be made and rules people had to follow to be right with God. It's not an enjoyable book to read— unless you understand grace! When you combine Leviticus with the nails of the cross and the crown of thorns, it reveals God's love, mercy, and grace toward His people.

Devotional: No Condemnation

If you still see God's Word as your source of condemnation, you have not yet grasped the mercy and grace that drips from its words onto its pages and into the hearts of those who are in Christ. You still haven't begun to see the seductive power of its truth.

Through faith, God's Word is no longer scary and intimidating. Instead of being a pronouncement of guilt, it becomes your story of mercy. Christ and the cross have removed the condemnation and made the law sweet to your eyes, your ears, and your mind. It has become a seductive force that will forever capture your heart.

WORKBOOK

Chapter Twenty Questions

Question: What comes to mind when you think about *the law*? Do you see God's law as constrictive and condemning or as the path to life, mercy, and redemption?

_____

_____

_____

_____

_____

_____

_____

_____

_____

_____

Question: Read 1 John 2:1. How has God acted on your behalf as your law, your judge, and your lawyer? How do you see His redemption in your life, both in your salvation and your sanctification?

_____

_____

_____

_____

_____

_____

_____

_____

_____

_____

Question: We can't understand true love on this earth until we've experienced God's love first. God's Word sets us free from our fears due to our confidence in knowing that His love is more powerful than that which torments us the most. What are some fears that you have when it comes to human relationships? What fears do you have regarding your relationship with God? How can a biblical understanding of God's love set you free from those fears?

_____

_____

_____

_____

_____

_____

_____

_____

_____

_____

_____

Action: Talk to a Christian who works in a legal field, such as law enforcement or the justice system. Ask them to help you contrast the role of an accuser vs. an advocate. What can their experience with the law teach you about what Christ has done for you? Why do they love man's law, and what insights can that give you into how to love God's law?

_____

_____

_____

_____

_____

_____

_____

_____

_____

_____

Chapter Twenty Notes

CHAPTER TWENTY-ONE

Sin and Shin—Kissing Trophies

I coached high school sports for about twenty years. I remember the feeling like it was yesterday when I won my first basketball championship as coach. I was coaching in South Carolina, and it would not be an understatement to say we were horrible when the season first started. I considered myself a good coach, and it was embarrassing— we were getting blown out by twenty, thirty, even forty points.

About halfway through the season, things started to click for our team. The games became closer. Then, we beat some teams that had killed us earlier in the year. We were on a winning streak, and we were sticking it to the other teams. We made it all the way to the championship, where we would face a team that had beaten us twice— first by forty-five points, then by fifteen.

The opposing team came into the game arrogant; they knew they had crushed us just five weeks before. As the score became closer and closer, they started to panic. They hadn't expected us to get better, but we did exactly that. The players bought in; I wised up as a coach, and we changed the way we played offense and defense.

Toward the end of the game, we started pulling away.

For the last three minutes, we were up by eight, ten, fifteen, then seventeen points. The clock counted down, the buzzer went off, and we all ran to the middle of the court, euphoric. Everyone was jumping up and down and hugging, excited because we had just won our first championship. Fans were coming up to talk to the players, and parents who had wanted me fired just a few weeks earlier were congratulating me. It was fun!

It was the most exciting moment of my coaching career. I still have the video of the game somewhere. Words cannot express how thrilling it was to celebrate this amazing victory with my players. It gave me tremendous joy to hold the trophy with them, and I still love talking about the whole experience. It was a perfect example of what happens when you play the game the right way.

That feeling is what David describes in this twenty-first stanza, titled "Sin and Shin," as he talks about how he feels about God's Word:

> **Princes** persecute me without a cause, but my heart stands in **awe** of Your word. I **rejoice** at Your word as one who finds great **treasure**. I hate and abhor lying, but I love Your law. Seven times a day I praise You, because of Your righteous judgments. Great peace have those who love Your law, and nothing causes them to stumble. LORD, I hope for Your salvation, and I do Your commandments. My soul keeps Your testimonies, and I love them exceedingly. I keep Your precepts and Your testimonies, for all my ways are before You.
> **—Psalm 119:161–168** *(NKJV, emphasis added)*

David felt like he had just won a huge victory, and God's Word was his trophy. Earthly trophies will rust, break, get lost, or be sold at garage sales. Though that championship win was one of the greatest moments of my coaching career, I no longer know where that trophy is.

That trophy pales in comparison to the one I desire the most—the crown of life (James 1:12, Revelation 2:10). That's the trophy I really want to kiss like professional athletes do when they win a championship.

Historical: Hebrew Word Study

Let's dig into the original Hebrew to better understand what David meant when he described himself as "one who finds great treasure" (v. 162). The Hebrew word translated as "princes" in verse 161 is *sar,* which means "chief, captain, general, prince, or ruler."[81] It carries the connotation of being a military leader, in charge of an army. The psalmist was under undeserved attack, with generals and princes coming after him.

The word translated as "awe," also in verse 161, is the Hebrew *pachad,* which means "to be startled or stunned."[82] Often, being startled or stunned takes your breath away. During the threat posed by these princes attacking and persecuting him, the psalmist was stunned and startled by God's Word.

In verse 162, the Hebrew word translated as "rejoice" is *suws,* meaning "to be bright, cheerful, glad."[83] On the heels of describing a battle, the psalmist declared he was stunned by God's Word, and it caused him to rejoice like one who finds great treasure.

This word "treasure," also in verse 162, is the Hebrew word *shalal,* which refers to booty or plunder as from war.[84] It's treasure you gain by defeating an enemy in battle. The psalmist described his love for God's Word by painting a picture of rulers and the spoils of victory.

A ruler's greatest possessions would be the spoils of war he had taken from his defeated enemies. These treasures would serve as a testimony to his prowess, power, and success, intimidating those around him. Finding spoil during a battle was one of the most exhilarating experiences an ancient-world ruler could have.

David's Greatest Spoil

To me, this is further evidence that David wrote Psalm 119. He understood what it meant to be a king, to face death in a battle, to have someone want to kill him, and to win that battle and find great victory. A great example is his battle with Goliath, in which David killed the Philistine champion with a slingshot (1 Samuel 17). David chopped off Goliath's head and brought it to Jerusalem as a trophy, which brought him great fame.

That trophy was exhilarating for David and he enjoyed his popularity among the people. Even though he achieved many great victories over his life, his greatest spoil, the treasure he cherished the most, was God's Word. Maybe we aren't out fighting literal giants and battles as David did, but with God's Word as our trophy, we can be victorious in times of calm as well as in life's battles.

Theological: Treasure on the Battlefield

When you see God's Word as an amazing trophy of victory, you will experience a joy that cannot be erased by the hardships of the battle. David makes comparisons to show how this precious treasure was a stunning find and the answer to his anxiety.

This is what happens when you see God's Word as your greatest spoil.

1. First, you will develop a hatred of untruth: "I hate and abhor lying, but I love Your law" (Psalm 119:163 NKJV).

If you truly see God's Word as your greatest treasure, there is nothing the world can offer you that you will love more than the Word of God.

The things you considered valuable before you

discovered the spoil of God's Word will no longer be appealing. Once you've tasted God's truth, falsehood loses its flavor. How does this happen? This tremendous prize you have discovered, the Word of God, leaves no room for falsehood in your life, stripping it of its power and appeal.

2. Second, when you see God's Word as your greatest spoil, it results in continuous praise to God: "Seven times a day I praise You, because of Your righteous judgments" (Psalm 119:164 NKJV).

This doesn't mean we need to praise God a certain number of times each day. It's about what occupies your thoughts and your daily routine.

This is a common theme in Scripture:

> *I will bless the LORD at all times; His praise shall continually be in my mouth.*
> **—Psalm 34:1** *(NKJV)*

> *Through him then let us continually offer up a sacrifice of praise to God, that is, the fruit of lips that acknowledge his name.*
> **—Hebrews 13:15**

To the psalmist, God's Word was such an incredible find, an amazing trophy of war, that he talked about it constantly. Even during sorrow and anxiety, all he could think about was this victory through God's Word.

To this day I love talking about that basketball team. It was such a great moment of victory; I love to tell the story. When we realize how great a trophy God's Word is, His stunning, awesome truth remains our main topic of conversation, our source of morality, the directive for our lifestyle, even when it seems like our burdens should dominate our every thought and word. His Word consumes our private thoughts and directs our decisions, and nothing can stop us from talking about it.

While we acknowledge the rough times we're going through—losing a loved one, uncertainties at work, difficulties with family or friends—we also acknowledge the treasure we have in God's Word. This treasure is so great that, even during anxiety and hardship, we have great spoil.

3. Third, when you see God's Word as your greatest spoil, you will experience incorruptible peace: "Great peace have those who love Your law, and nothing causes them to stumble. LORD, I hope for Your salvation, and I do Your commandments" (Psalm 119:165–166 NKJV).

The world around us is designed to steal our peace. It's designed to promise us hope, only to break our hearts when fails to deliver. But the peace that is created when we find the spoil of God's Word is something the world can neither duplicate nor take away.

When God's Word is your greatest spoil, no threat, no defeat, no danger can destroy the peace that comes from the reality that your hope for salvation is in the Lord. Its wholly satisfying effect on your heart and soul is this unwavering peace, even in the face of war or impending death.

Paul had such an amazing understanding of the concept of peace that it blows my mind. As he wrote in his letter to the Philippians:

Do not be anxious about anything, but in everything by prayer and supplication with thanksgiving let your requests be made known to God. And the peace of God, which surpasses all understanding, will guard your hearts and your minds in Christ Jesus.

—Philippians 4:6–7

4. Fourth, when God's Word is your greatest spoil, you will take pleasure in obedience: "My soul keeps Your testimonies, and I love them exceedingly. I keep Your precepts and Your testimonies, for all my ways are before You" (Psalm 119:167–168 NKJV).

You likely keep any trophies or items you value on display. You remember them and keep them safe. Every time you see these valuable items, you're taken back to the moment you first stumbled upon them.

When God's Word is our greatest spoil, we find fulfillment and comfort in obeying it and joy in following it. Even during times of sorrow and anxiety, our hearts are inclined to cling to this treasure, this grace that took our breath away amid the battle. Our obedience to the spoil of God's Word brings unbelievable satisfaction because it keeps the memory and joy of that moment we first discovered truth fresh in our hearts and minds.

Save Your Kisses

When Paul addressed this issue with the Corinthians, he knew they were familiar with the concept of competing to win a prize in an athletic contest. Ancient Corinth was host to the Isthmian Games; a festival of athletic events similar to the Olympics.[85] Paul therefore used this concept of pursuing an athletic prize to help the Corinthians understand how they should pursue the real prize:

> *Every athlete exercises self-control in all things. They do it to receive a perishable wreath, but we an imperishable. So I do not run aimlessly; I do not box as one beating the air. But I discipline my body and keep it under control, lest after preaching to others I myself should be disqualified.*
> **—1 Corinthians 9:25-27**

This image Paul presents of an athlete running and

boxing with discipline and purpose is synonymous with pursuing a love for God's Word. We do whatever it takes to find this great treasure that will give us the crown of life (James 1:12). It's a picture of pursuing the ultimate trophy that any of us could ever receive.

Imagine the feeling when we celebrate that ultimate victory through God's Word as a result of hearing and receiving the gospel. We'll finally come face to face with our Savior, and He'll say, "You won! All the things you went through—your physical, emotional, and spiritual struggles, your hardships, your training—were worthwhile. You found the truth of the gospel, and you have won the crown of life."

Can you imagine the euphoria we will feel in that day? All our greatest moments on this earth will pale in comparison. Nothing will compare to that moment when we celebrate in the middle of the court with Jesus and His church. We won!

Devotional: Your Greatest Moment

I love what Paul wrote to Timothy, his apprentice, toward the end of Paul's life. It's similar to what he wrote to the Corinthians:

> *I have fought the good fight, I have finished the race, I have kept the faith. Henceforth there is laid up for me the crown of righteousness, which the Lord, the righteous judge, will award to me on that day, and not only to me but also to all who have loved his appearing.*
>
> *—2 Timothy 4:7–8*

This is the trophy David was talking about, the spoil that brought him a love of truth and incorruptible peace and taught him to praise God continuously and take pleasure in obedience.

What would you consider your greatest trophy? What would you consider your greatest moment? I've spent a good deal of time reflecting on these questions myself. My greatest moment wasn't that championship or the day I got married or the day we planted our church. *It was the moment I found the most valuable spoil on earth: God's Word.*

WORKBOOK

Chapter Twenty-One Questions

Question: Describe a time when you experienced the elation of victory through winning a literal trophy or being part of a tremendous accomplishment. What emotions did you experience? What are some tangible trophies that you consider prized possessions and why are they special to you?

_____

_____

_____

_____

_____

_____

_____

_____

_____

Question: Is God's Word like a trophy and a treasure to you? Why or why not? How does it line up in your affections with the greatest moments and achievements and possessions in your life? Would others say you are obsessed with the Word the way that a victor might be with his spoils or a lover with his beloved?

_____

_____

_____

_____

_____

_____

_____

_____

_____

_____

Question: How have you experienced the supernatural peace that comes from God and His Word? In what ways is this peace different from peace based on human ideals, psychological study, or perfectly engineered circumstances?

_____

_____

_____

_____

_____

_____

_____

_____

_____

_____

_____

_____

Action: In past eras when books were very scarce, God's Word was often literally a treasure with gilt-edged pages, jeweled covers, and expensive illustrations. While Christians should not worship the book itself, how can you, in this era of Bible apps and inexpensive New Testaments, show that you cherish the contents of this book? Make a list of some practical ways that you will treasure God's Word in your home and throughout each part of your day.

_____

_____

_____

_____

_____

_____

_____

_____

Chapter Twenty-One Notes

_____

_____

_____

_____

_____

_____

_____

_____

_____

_____

_____

_____

_____

_____

_____

_____

_____

_____

_____

_____

_____

_____

_____

CHAPTER TWENTY-TWO

Taw—Coda

According to the Merriam-Webster dictionary, a coda is "a concluding musical section that is formally distinct from the main structure" or "a concluding part of a literary or dramatic work." It is "something that serves to round out, conclude, or summarize and usually has its own interest.[86]

This final stanza of Psalm 119, titled "Taw" is the coda for the entire psalm. It serves as a conclusion for the psalmist's overall message while still being its own distinct section. It ties everything together but still leaves us with something new, something additional to reflect on.

As such, this last stanza has a distinctly different structure from the preceding twenty-one songs that make up the album that is Psalm 119. We've seen how the first verse or two in each stanza gives the theme of that section, and the remaining verses expand on that theme. This time, it's very different. The first two verses are repeated over and over to the end—not necessarily word for word but in concept.

Let my cry come before You, O LORD; give me

understanding according to Your word. Let my supplication come before You; deliver me according to Your word. My lips shall utter praise, for You teach me Your statutes. My tongue shall speak of Your word, for all Your commandments are righteousness. Let Your hand become my help, for I have chosen Your precepts. I long for Your salvation, O LORD, and Your law is my delight. Let my soul live, and it shall praise You; and let Your judgments help me. I have gone astray like a lost sheep; seek Your servant, for I do not forget Your commandments.

—Psalm 119:169–176 (NKJV)

The psalmist was clearly emotional when he wrote this. He had just concluded this amazing masterpiece. The more I study Psalm 119, the more awestruck I am at what an incredible composer David was. The level of attention to structure and meaning, the careful choice and placement of words, the repetition of words similar to the first word but just slightly different—it's all so masterful.

At the very end of this final stanza, David sets forth a theme driven home by all the other themes he's covered in the first twenty-one songs. There was no other place for him to end up than right here; this is the coda of his relationship with God's Word. It's meant to give us an emotional sense of finality.

The final feeling with which the psalmist concludes is total reliance upon God. It's not his discipline in God's Word, his knowledge, or his ability to make sure he stays on God's path—none of that is in the coda. Instead, the psalmist focuses on his helplessness. He needed God in every letter, every syllable, every word, every line, every stanza, and every song.

Devotional: Four Prayers of Reliance

Having such a different structure in the coda reinforces that concept. In fact, it's such a different structure that I've decided to dispense with the historical, theological, devotional format for this chapter. The way the psalmist wrote this stanza, there's really only one application: devotional.

The coda is pure devotion, and it is centered on four prayers of reliance upon God.

1. The first prayer of reliance is a cry for understanding: "Let my *cry* come before You, O LORD; give me *understanding* according to Your word. Let my supplication come before You; deliver me according to Your word" (Psalm 119:169 NKJV, emphasis added).

The word translated as "cry" in verse 169 is the Hebrew *rinnah,* which refers to a shrill sound, a sound of joy, gladness, proclamation, or rejoicing.[87] In that same verse, the Hebrew word translated as "understanding" is *biyn,* which means "to separate mentally or to discern."[88]

The psalmist cried out to God, begging Him to help him see the world through the eyes of God. Notice this is the first request the psalmist makes in the coda. He's already cried out for understanding multiple times in this psalm, but it's such an important request that he continues to make it right to the very end.

The psalmist didn't understand what he was reading in God's Word. He couldn't completely grasp it, so he asked God for discernment, for understanding. He recognized everything else he did hinged upon God enlightening him with wisdom.

The only way you can love God's Word is if God supernaturally intervenes and enlightens you as you read. Reading it in your own strength and wisdom doesn't benefit you at all. You must be visited by the Holy Spirit, who wrote it.

Paul prayed for this for the Ephesians:

I do not cease to give thanks for you, remembering you in my prayers, that the God of our Lord Jesus Christ, the Father of glory, may give you the Spirit of wisdom and of revelation in the knowledge of him, having the eyes of your hearts enlightened, that you may know what is the hope to which he has called you, what are the riches of his glorious inheritance in the saints, and what is the immeasurable greatness of his power toward us who believe, according to the working of his great might.

—Ephesians 1:16–19

Paul was saying the only way you can truly understand how great salvation is if the Holy Spirit enlightens the eyes of your heart.

2. The second prayer of reliance in the coda is a plea for deliverance: "Let my *supplication* come before You; *deliver* me according to Your word. My lips shall utter praise, for You teach me Your statutes. My tongue shall speak of Your word, for all Your commandments are righteousness" (Psalm 119:170–172 NKJV, emphasis added).

The Hebrew word translated as "supplication" in verse 170 is *techinnah,* which is a request for favor and grace.[89] In that same verse, the word translated as "deliver" is the Hebrew *natsal,* meaning "to snatch away or pluck out."[90]

The psalmist needed God's grace, and he needed God to snatch him away from where he was at the time, to pluck him out of the darkness. David recognized that understanding God's Word leads to a desire to be delivered from evil. If you do not have God's Word in your heart, you won't see a reason to fall out of love with the world. But because the psalmist had been given understanding, he could see the world through God's eyes, and he knew he didn't want to be a part of what wicked people were doing. He knew he needed God's grace and for God to deliver him from that mess.

Once the eyes of your heart have been enlightened (Ephesians 1:18), you begin to plead for deliverance. In fact, Jesus taught that this was one of the ingredients of a good prayer when he prayed, "And lead us not into temptation, but deliver us from evil" (Matthew 6:13 ESV).

Jesus knew evil would surround us and He tells us to come to Him to ask that we would not be tempted by it or overwhelmed with it. When the eyes of your heart are focused on God's Word, you are better able to see the evil and darkness around you.

The result of God answering these prayers is an overflow of praise founded upon the words of life. The thought of God's deliverance thrills David so much that the only response is a natural outpouring of gratitude and praise.

3. The third prayer of reliance in the coda is a request for unceasing help: "Let Your hand become my help, for I have chosen Your precepts" (Psalm 119:173 NKJV).

David realized salvation is not only contingent upon God enlightening us and plucking us out of the darkness but upon God keeping us.

The only way we can persevere as saints and continue to walk with God is with His hand on us the whole time. Salvation and redemption are entirely His work from start to finish. There can be no reliance upon self.

David therefore always asked God to keep His hand on him. He knew even after God delivered him, he couldn't continue with God's Word unless God kept him with His hand. It's like when you cross the street with a child. What happens to your grip? It gets tighter because you know your child is prone to wander. That's exactly what David was asking God to do for him.

Paul had this to say about God keeping His hands on us:

> *For I am sure that neither death nor life, nor angels nor rulers, nor things present nor things to come, nor powers, nor height nor depth, nor anything else in all creation, will be able to separate us from the love of God in Christ Jesus our Lord.*
> **—Romans 8:38–39**

4. The fourth prayer of reliance in the coda expresses a longing for salvation: "I long for Your salvation, O LORD, and Your law is my delight. Let my soul live, and it shall praise You; and let Your judgments help me" (Psalm 119:174–175 NKJV).

The other three prayers focus on the now, but this prayer turns to the eternal.

Salvation is different from deliverance. Deliverance is for now—deliverance from our sins, from the evil of others, from the consequences of our mistakes. Salvation is eternal. The psalmist's heart was focused on heaven, looking outward and upward.

As he longed for salvation, the psalmist recognized only God could bring it to fruition. He was completely reliant upon God keeping His promise. After twenty-one songs about how much he loved God's Word, he realized he was completely helpless without God.

These four prayers are about total dependence upon God. They involve a total rejection of self-confidence, self-help, self-discipline, and any trust in your own flesh or will.

The Final Verse

> I have gone astray like a lost sheep; seek Your servant, for I do not forget Your commandments.
>
> **—Psalm 119:176** *(NKJV)*

The last verse of this psalm keeps ringing in my head. The psalmist who clearly loved God's Word admitted he constantly wandered and strayed. He asked God to seek after him and find him, even when he didn't want to be found.

We must never forget our propensity for sin and our need of God's mercy and grace. No matter how much we read God's Word, it's important we pray and memorize our walk with God because we are still prone to wander. False spiritual pride creeps in and pollutes our relationship with God's Word and God's people. When we feel like we've arrived in our relationship with God, we must remember we are sheep who like to stray and beg God to come look for us.

David's confession and his passion for God's Word are supernatural. They are not achieved by human effort. It's the Holy Spirit infusing him—and us—with life and supernatural passion for truth. It's a fitting conclusion for a masterpiece of a psalm.

Prone to Wander

Be honest. As we've progressed through the twenty-two chapters of this book, and learned where we need to be in our relationship with God's Word, have you found yourself a little intimidated? Have you been discouraged at times, thinking about how far you are from where you need to be with God's Word?

As I've looked back on my journal entries from when I first studied Psalm 119, I've seen how I struggled with that same burden. But you know what? I am confident David felt the very same way as he concluded this masterpiece. The evidence is the final verse!

There is great comfort in admitting you're prone to wander. Once you get to that point, the pressure comes off. You know you cannot develop a love for God's Word unless the Good Shepherd comes and finds you first. That is the only true path to loving God's Word—God's relentless desire to go after His wandering sheep.

Jesus said:

> *What do you think? If a man has a hundred sheep, and one of them has gone astray, does he not leave the ninety-nine on the mountains and go in search of the one that went*

astray? And if he finds it, truly, I say to you, he rejoices over it more than over the ninety-nine that never went astray. So it is not the will of my Father who is in heaven that one of these little ones should perish.

—Matthew 18:12-14

Do you see how this theme repeats throughout the Bible from the Old Testament to the New Testament? David described himself as a sheep who went astray and needed to be found, and Jesus made it clear that God will always go after His wandering sheep.

A passionate relationship with God and His Word starts the way David ended Psalm 119. If you're not satisfied with where you are with God's Word, you need to know it won't improve simply because of your resolve to do so or because you get good at religion. Being a lost sheep found by the Good Shepherd is what births a passion for the truth.

The Good Shepherd left heaven to come and get His wandering sheep, the ones who didn't love truth. He came, He enlightened them, and He plucked them from danger. He helps them every step of the way and gives them eyes for eternity.

Not only did He leave heaven, He came to earth to die for those wandering sheep. They were so lost that He knew the only way He was going to get those sheep back was by giving His life for them. That's how badly He wanted those sheep back in His fold. He died for us, His wandering sheep, so that we could be saved and fall in love with His Word.

All we like sheep have gone astray; we have turned, every one, to his own way; and the LORD has laid on Him the iniquity of us all.

—Isaiah 53:6 (NKJV)

We have all gone astray, and God found us, took our sin and laid it on His son, Jesus, the Living Word of God!

As we conclude our journey through Psalm 119, our adventure in learning how to love God's Word, I'm giving you the final step. I invite you into the comfort of confessing, "I am a straying sheep, desiring to be found by the Father." Through Christ, God has come, He has sought you, He is enlightening you, and He is putting His hand on you and pointing you toward eternity. May He give you a passion for truth and His Word. Isn't it amazing? Our journey to learn how to fall in love with God's Word starts right where Psalm 119 ends!

WORKBOOK

Chapter Twenty-Two Questions

Question: When do you most recognize your dependence on God? When are you most tempted to go it alone? What is your default—depending on God or trying to live the Christian life in your own strength?

_____

_____

_____

_____

_____

_____

_____

_____

_____

_____

Question: What are some things in the Bible that you find confusing, conflicting, or difficult? Have you asked God for understanding in these areas? Commit to seeking His wisdom about all your scriptural questions.

_____

_____

_____

_____

_____

_____

_____

_____

_____

_____

Question: What are some areas where you are prone to wander? How can the power of God's Word and prayer for His deliverance from evil be tools to help you when you are tempted? How have you experienced God as your Keeper, the one on whom you depend entirely for your righteousness, deliverance, and salvation?

_____

_____

_____

_____

_____

_____

_____

_____

_____

_____

_____

_____

Action: Listen to a recording of "Come Thou Fount of Every Blessing," paying particular attention to the final verse where the author says he is "prone to wander." Can you sing this verse as a prayer? Reflecting on all you have learned through Psalm 119, like David write out your own poem, song, or journal entry of praise to God for His amazing Word!

_____

_____

_____

_____

_____

_____

_____

_____

_____

Chapter Twenty-Two Notes

CONCLUSION

A Continuing Journey

Congratulations! You've just completed an in-depth study of the longest chapter in the Bible. Psalm 119 is a treasure trove of insights into God's Word and of the benefits it brings to us. I hope this study has helped you grow in your love for God's Word and your understanding of why it is so important for you to have a relationship with the Word of God.

Loving God's Word gives you a foundation of truth, enabling you to separate yourself from the lies and emptiness of this world and to stop clinging to temporary things. It frees you to live as God has called you to live and to walk the path He has called you to walk. His Word provides the light you need every step of the way.

Even in the darkest times of your life, your relationship with God's Word will sustain you. As His Word continues to work in you, you experience the process of redemption, making you more and more like Christ. Instead of focusing on your circumstances, your eyes are fixed on eternity.

It's important to remember the Word of God is not only Scripture; it's Jesus Himself. He took on our sins, agreeing to pay the debt we couldn't pay, and secured our salvation through His death on the cross. Because of

Jesus, we can have a relationship with God and His Word and experience the confidence of knowing we will spend eternity in heaven with Him.

Jesus' righteousness has become our own, freeing us to live lives of gratitude and obedience. Instead of seeing God's Word as a source of judgment and condemnation, we see it as filled with promises, encouragement, hope, and necessary rebuke. We no longer fear the day of judgment and instead look forward to the completion of our salvation in Christ on that day.

As we continue to meditate on God's Word, filling our hearts and minds with it, we will continue to draw closer to its Author, learning more about His character and His great love for us. We will eventually come to a point where His Word becomes our greatest trophy, our ultimate prize.

Though we tend to wander from God's Word, like sheep who have gone astray, we can take comfort in the fact that God will always come find us, drawing our hearts back to Him and setting us back on His path.

We have concluded our journey through Psalm 119, but our journey of growing in our love for God's Word continues. Until we are at home with Heavenly Dad, there will always be room for growth in our relationship with Him and His Word. I pray the insights you have gained from this study have given you a hunger and a thirst for more of God's Word and that you will continue to dig deep into the riches of Scripture.

About the Author

Joe is the founding pastor of GraceLife Church (www.gracelifesrq.com) in Sarasota, Florida. He holds a bachelor's degree in biblical studies and another in pastoral studies, as well as a master's degree in theology.

After beginning vocational ministry at age 18, Joe spent his first twenty-two years of ministry as a youth pastor and outreach pastor in three different churches. He coached high school football and basketball for nearly twenty years.

In 2008, Joe founded Mobilepreacher.org (www.mobilepreacher.org), an organization designed to help seasoned ministers create ministries that might not fit inside traditional church walls. He is also the founder and executive director of the Nightlife Center in Sarasota (www.nightlifecenter.org) and the author of *The GraceLife: What Philippians Teaches Us About Loving One Another Relentlessly.*

Joe is husband to Laura and father to Ben. You can find him on Twitter (@mobilepreacher), Instagram (Mobilepreacher) and on Facebook (facebook.com/Mobilepreacher).

REFERENCES

Notes

[1] Strong, James. "H8549: tamim." *A Concise Dictionary of the Words in the Greek Testament and the Hebrew Bible.* Faithlife, 2009.

[2] Goodrick, Edward W. and John Kohlenberger. "Hebrew to English section, number 897." *The Strongest NIV Exhaustive Concordance.* Zondervan, 2004.

[3] Strong, "H5341: natsar." *A Concise Dictionary of the Words in the Greek Testament and the Hebrew Bible.* Faithlife, 2009.

[4] Strong, James. "H1875: darash." *A Concise Dictionary of the Words in the Greek Testament and the Hebrew Bible.* Faithlife, 2009.

[5] Strong, James. "H954: buwsh." *A Concise Dictionary of the Words in the Greek Testament and the Hebrew Bible.* Faithlife, 2009.

[6] Strong, James. "H3034: yadah." *A Concise Dictionary of the Words in the Greek Testament and the Hebrew Bible.* Faithlife, 2009.

[7] Strong, James. "H2135: zakah." *A Concise Dictionary of the Words in the Greek Testament and the Hebrew Bible.* Faithlife, 2009.

[8] Strong, James. "H8104: shamar." *A Concise Dictionary of the Words in the Greek Testament and the Hebrew Bible.* Faithlife, 2009.

[9] Strong, James. "H7686: shagah." *A Concise Dictionary of the Words in the Greek Testament and the Hebrew Bible.* Faithlife, 2009.

[10] Strong, James. "H1580: gamal." *A Concise Dictionary of the Words in the Greek Testament and the Hebrew Bible.* Faithlife, 2009.

[11] Strong, "H1580: gamal."

[12] Strong, James. "H6381: pala." *A Concise Dictionary of the Words in the Greek Testament and the Hebrew Bible.* Faithlife, 2009.

[13] Strong, James. "H1616: ger." *A Concise Dictionary of the Words in the Greek Testament and the Hebrew Bible.* Faithlife, 2009.

[14] Strong, James. "H5641: sathar." *A Concise Dictionary of the Words in the Greek Testament and the Hebrew Bible.* Faithlife, 2009.

[15] Strong, James. "H6083: aphar." *A Concise Dictionary of the Words in the Greek Testament and the Hebrew Bible.* Faithlife, 2009.

[16] Strong, James. "H1811: dalaph." *A Concise Dictionary of the Words in the Greek Testament and the Hebrew Bible.* Faithlife, 2009.

[17] Strong, James. "H1692: dabaq." *A Concise Dictionary of the Words in the Greek Testament and the Hebrew Bible.* Faithlife, 2009.

[18] Strong, James. "H7337: rachab." *A Concise Dictionary of the Words in the Greek Testament and the Hebrew Bible.* Faithlife, 2009.

[19] Strong, James. "H5410: nathiyb." *A Concise Dictionary of the Words in the Greek Testament and the Hebrew Bible.* Faithlife, 2009.

[20] Strong, James. "H5186: natah." *A Concise Dictionary of the Words in the Greek Testament and the Hebrew Bible.* Faithlife, 2009.

[21] Strong, James. "H6969: quwn." *A Concise Dictionary of the Words*

in the Greek Testament and the Hebrew Bible. Faithlife, 2009.

[22] Strong, James. "H7337: rachab." *A Concise Dictionary of the Words in the Greek Testament and the Hebrew Bible.* Faithlife, 2009.

[23] Strong, James. "H954: buwsh." *A Concise Dictionary of the Words in the Greek Testament and the Hebrew Bible.* Faithlife, 2009.

[24] Photograph used with permissions from Inside BruCrew Life. insidebrucrewlife.com.

[25] Strong, James. "H2506: cheleq." *A Dictionary of the Words in the Greek Testament and the Hebrew Bible.* Faithlife, 2009.

[26] Roberts, John. Quoted in "'I Wish You Bad Luck.' Read Supreme Court Justice John Roberts' Unconventional Speech to His Son's Graduating Class." By Katie Reilly. July 5, 2017. *TIME Magazine.* https://time.com/4845150/chief-justice-john-roberts-commencement-speech-transcript/.

[27] Strong, James. "H2896: towb." *A Dictionary of the Words in the Greek Testament and the Hebrew Bible.* Faithlife, 2009.

[28] Strong, James. "H6030: anah." *A Dictionary of the Words in the Greek Testament and the Hebrew Bible.* Faithlife, 2009.

[29] Strong, James. "H6213: asah." *A Dictionary of the Words in the Greek Testament and the Hebrew Bible.* Faithlife, 2009.

[30] Strong, James. "H3559: kuwn." *A Dictionary of the Words in the Greek Testament and the Hebrew Bible.* Faithlife, 2009.

[31] Strong, James. "H8055: samach." *A Dictionary of the Words in the Greek Testament and the Hebrew Bible.* Faithlife, 2009.

[32] Strong, James. "H3615: kalah." *A Dictionary of the Words in the Greek Testament and the Hebrew Bible.* Faithlife, 2009.

[33] Strong, James. "H8668: teshuah." *A Dictionary of the Words in the Greek Testament and the Hebrew Bible.* Faithlife, 2009.

[34] Strong, James. "H565: imrah." *A Dictionary of the Words in the Greek Testament and the Hebrew Bible.* Faithlife, 2009.

[35] McWhorter, Harold. "Sin Will Take You Farther." *Goin' In Style.* Homeward Bound Music (BMI), 1988.

[36] Strong, James. "H7342: rachab." *A Dictionary of the Words in the Greek Testament and the Hebrew Bible.* Faithlife, 2009.

[37] Strong, James. "H8064: shameh." *A Dictionary of the Words in the Greek Testament and the Hebrew Bible.* Faithlife, 2009.

[38] Strong, James. "H1755: dor." *A Dictionary of the Words in the Greek Testament and the Hebrew Bible.* Faithlife, 2009.

[39] Strong, James. "H5975: amad." *A Dictionary of the Words in the Greek Testament and the Hebrew Bible.* Faithlife, 2009.

[40] Strong, James. "H8191: shashua." *A Dictionary of the Words in the Greek Testament and the Hebrew Bible.* Faithlife, 2009.

[41] Strong, James. "H995: biyn." *A Dictionary of the Words in the Greek Testament and the Hebrew Bible.* Faithlife, 2009.

[42] Strong, James. "H7342: rachab." *A Dictionary of the Words in the Greek Testament and the Hebrew Bible.* Faithlife, 2009.

[43] "Bait and Switch." *Merriam-Webster Dictionary.* https://www.merriam-webster.com/dictionary/bait%20and%20switch.

[44] Storms, Sam. "Sweeter Than Honey to My Mouth! (Psalm 119)." *Enjoying God.* https://www.samstorms.com/all-articles/post/sweeter-than-honey-to-my-mouth--psalm-119-.

[45] Strong, James. "H7881: siychah." *A Dictionary of the Words in the Greek Testament and the Hebrew Bible.* Faithlife, 2009.

[46] Strong, James. "H3117: yowm." *A Dictionary of the Words in the Greek Testament and the Hebrew Bible.* Faithlife, 2009.

[47] Strong, James. "H2449: chakam." *A Dictionary of the Words in the Greek Testament and the Hebrew Bible.* Faithlife, 2009.

[48] Strong, James. "H3607: kala." *A Dictionary of the Words in the Greek Testament and the Hebrew Bible.* Faithlife, 2009.

[49] Strong, James. "H5493: cuwr." *A Dictionary of the Words in the Greek Testament and the Hebrew Bible.* Faithlife, 2009.

[50] Strong, James. "H2441: chek." *A Dictionary of the Words in the Greek Testament and the Hebrew Bible.* Faithlife, 2009.

[51] Strong, James. "H8130: sane." *A Dictionary of the Words in the Greek Testament and the Hebrew Bible.* Faithlife, 2009.

[52] Strong, James. "H5216: ner." *A Dictionary of the Words in the Greek Testament and the Hebrew Bible.* Faithlife, 2009.

[53] Strong, James. "H7272: regel." *A Dictionary of the Words in the Greek Testament and the Hebrew Bible.* Faithlife, 2009.

[54] Strong, James. "H215: owr." *A Dictionary of the Words in the Greek Testament and the Hebrew Bible.* Faithlife, 2009.

[55] Strong, James. "H5410: nathiyb." *A Dictionary of the Words in the Greek Testament and the Hebrew Bible.* Faithlife, 2009.

[56] Strong, James. "H5588: ceeph." *A Dictionary of the Words in the Greek Testament and the Hebrew Bible.* Faithlife, 2009.

[57] Strong, James. "H5643: cether." *A Dictionary of the Words in the Greek Testament and the Hebrew Bible.* Faithlife, 2009.

[58] Strong, James. "H4043: magen." *A Dictionary of the Words in the Greek Testament and the Hebrew Bible.* Faithlife, 2009.

[59] "Massive Granite Slab—'100 Feet by 100 Feet'—Falls Off El Capitan in Yosemite, Killing 1." September 28, 2017. *Chicago Tribune.* https://www.chicagotribune.com/nation-world/ct-yosemite-rock-fall-20170927-story.html.

[60] Strong, James. "H4941: mishpat." *A Dictionary of the Words in the Greek Testament and the Hebrew Bible.* Faithlife, 2009.

[61] Strong, James. "H6664: tsedeq." *A Dictionary of the Words in the Greek Testament and the Hebrew Bible.* Faithlife, 2009.

[62] Strong, James. "H6148: arab." *A Dictionary of the Words in the Greek Testament and the Hebrew Bible.* Faithlife, 2009.

[63] Photograph used with permissions from Inside BruCrew Life. insidebrucrewlife.com.

[64] Strong, James. "H6382: pele." *A Dictionary of the Words in the Greek Testament and the Hebrew Bible.* Faithlife, 2009.

[65] Strong, James. "H6608: pethach." *A Dictionary of the Words in the Greek Testament and the Hebrew Bible.* Faithlife, 2009.

[66] Strong, James. "H217: uwr." *A Dictionary of the Words in the Greek Testament and the Hebrew Bible.* Faithlife, 2009.

[67] Strong, James. "H7602: shaaph." *A Dictionary of the Words in the Greek Testament and the Hebrew Bible.* Faithlife, 2009.

[68] Strong, James. "H6662: tsaddiyq." *A Dictionary of the Words in the Greek Testament and the Hebrew Bible.* Faithlife, 2009.

[69] Strong, James. "H3477: yashar." *A Dictionary of the Words in the Greek Testament and the Hebrew Bible.* Faithlife, 2009.

[70] Strong, James. "H6680: tsavah." *A Dictionary of the Words in the Greek Testament and the Hebrew Bible*. Faithlife, 2009.

[71] Strong, James. "Strong's H7121–qara'." In Blue Letter Bible. https://www.blueletterbible.org/lang/lexicon/lexicon.cfm?Strongs= H7121&t=KJV.

[72] Strong, James. "H6030: anah." *A Dictionary of the Words in the Greek Testament and the Hebrew Bible*. Faithlife, 2009.

[73] Strong, James. "H3467: yasha." *A Dictionary of the Words in the Greek Testament and the Hebrew Bible*. Faithlife, 2009.

[74] Shakespeare, William. *King Henry VI: Part II*. Act 2, Scene 1, Lines 73–74. In *The Works of Shakespeare* (Vol. 3). R. Tyas, 1843, p. 297.

[75] Strong, James. "H7200: ra'ah." *A Dictionary of the Words in the Greek Testament and the Hebrew Bible*. Faithlife, 2009.

[76] Strong, James. "H6040: oiny." *A Dictionary of the Words in the Greek Testament and the Hebrew Bible*. Faithlife, 2009.

[77] Strong, James. "H2502: chalats." *A Dictionary of the Words in the Greek Testament and the Hebrew Bible*. Faithlife, 2009.

[78] Strong, James. "H7378: riyb." *A Dictionary of the Words in the Greek Testament and the Hebrew Bible*. Faithlife, 2009.

[79] Strong, James. "H7379: riyb." *A Dictionary of the Words in the Greek Testament and the Hebrew Bible*. Faithlife, 2009.

[80] Strong, James. "H1350: ga'al." *A Dictionary of the Words in the Greek Testament and the Hebrew Bible*. Faithlife, 2009.

[81] Strong, James. "H8269: sar." *A Dictionary of the Words in the Greek Testament and the Hebrew Bible*. Faithlife, 2009.

[82] Strong, James. "H6342: pachad." *A Dictionary of the Words in the Greek Testament and the Hebrew Bible.* Faithlife, 2009.

[83] Strong, James. "H7797: suws." *A Dictionary of the Words in the Greek Testament and the Hebrew Bible.* Faithlife, 2009.

[84] Strong, James. "H7998: shalal." *A Dictionary of the Words in the Greek Testament and the Hebrew Bible.* Faithlife, 2009.

[85] "Isthmian Games: Ancient Greek Festival." *Encyclopaedia Britannica.* https://www.britannica.com/sports/Isthmian-Games.

[86] "Coda." *Merriam-Webster Dictionary.* https://www.merriam-webster.com/dictionary/coda.

[87] Strong, James. "H7440: rinnah." *A Dictionary of the Words in the Greek Testament and the Hebrew Bible.* Faithlife, 2009.

[88] Strong, James. "H995: biyn." *A Dictionary of the Words in the Greek Testament and the Hebrew Bible.* Faithlife, 2009.

[89] Strong, James. "H8467: techinnah." *A Dictionary of the Words in the Greek Testament and the Hebrew Bible.* Faithlife, 2009.

[90] Strong, James. "H5337: natsal." *A Dictionary of the Words in the Greek Testament and the Hebrew Bible.* Faithlife, 2009.

Made in the USA
Las Vegas, NV
09 March 2022

45297551R00184